T0162657

Eddie

GROWING UP IN THE EARLY 20TH CENTURY

EDWARD LANDERS

Order this book online at www.trafford.com
or email orders@trafford.com

Most Trafford titles are also available at major online book retailers.

This is an autobiography. The attitudes portrayed therein are wholly due to the author.

Printed in the United States of America.

ISBN: 978-1-4669-6736-6 (sc)
ISBN: 978-1-4669-6735-9 (e)

Trafford rev. 11/08/2012

 www.trafford.com

North America & international
toll-free: 1 888 232 4444 (USA & Canada)
phone: 250 383 6864 ♦ fax: 812 355 4082

For Mom.

You taught me well and I remember each
and every one of those lessons.

Cover designed by Lisa Pride, a budding
artist from Barrington, Illinois.

Preface

Some time ago I entertained the idea of writing a book that documented the time I spent on active duty in the Navy. The name of the book was Smooth. I wrote in order to leave a little something for my daughter, Laura, who spent most of that time with me but was much too young to remember anything that had transpired in the first eight years of her life. After she had read the book she commented, "That was nice but how about telling us about your childhood; about the time before your life in the Navy?"

When I had given it a little thought I realized that I had missed knowing much about my parent's life. It would have been nice to be able to refer to a book written by my father or mother about their lives. I had always enjoyed the little snippets related by them about incidents that had happened to them. Now that they are gone most information concerning them is gone also. Other than a few dry statistics that well of information had suddenly dried up forever. The realization that information of that sort was ephemeral and was interesting to future generations prompted me to write the current book.

I've always thought that a well developed sense of humor is one of the more valuable things a person can possess along with a keen sense of curiosity. It is a vital attribute to be able to laugh at one's self. People who do not possess that attribute tend to be dry, humorless husks who are not pleasant company. That being said, every effort was made to present the material in this book with a sense of humor, wry at times, tongue-in-cheek at times but always with the goal of making the reader smile or even laugh.

All through the book I have tried to contrast the slower pace of life and the freedom that children and young people had during that time period with today's fast paced, controlled life style. Children of the 1930s and 40s seemed to have more imagination than kids do today, not due so much to any genetic differences but out of necessity. Most of the kids I grew up with simply didn't have the toys that abound today and their parents were, by and large, too concerned with jobs either inside or outside of the home to pay much attention to them. As a result their kids were forced to use their own ingenuity to create play situations.

Eddie is the first in a series of books portraying the life of a young person born into a family in the Midwest in the early 20th century. Eddie was born in Terre Haute, Indiana in 1936. He grew up during the war years of World War II and survived a number of moves around the United States along with the normal fistfights and bullies that can be found anywhere and life in general. Eddie is just like any number of kids who grew up in that era but, unlike some, he was independent and fierce in demanding his liberty. The way he handled controversy is interesting and humorous. Eddie was a Libertarian before he ever knew what one was. Readers can readily identify and emphasize with the young boy who tries unsuccessfully to avoid controversy and fights and ultimately has to deal with the dragons that we all have to deal with at sometime in our lives.

If there is one overriding theme that trickles throughout the book it is that of freedom, the ability to choose what you wish to do without interference from government, family or friends. I leave it up to the reader to solve the dichotomy that necessarily exists between a person who values, above all, their freedom and the same person who sacrifices that same freedom for a life in the military, perhaps the one career that has less freedom than any other. The author solved that issue easily by virtue of realizing that the ultimate freedom was that attained in the cockpit of an airplane. He has spent his life in pursuing that freedom, warring fiercely against those who would set limits on that particular freedom.

Imagination is a wonderful gift to mankind. Used properly it can amuse and enthrall for hours. Used improperly it can curtail thought processes through fear. Kids in the period of this book use their fertile imaginations to transport them to other places, other times, other situations. They played "cops and robbers", "cowboys and Indians", "house" and "dolls" with little or no toys other than sticks or whatever came to hand to embellish their imaginative adventurous forays. Television had not been perfected yet and was not available to the masses even as rudimentary as it was then. Kids (and adults) relied on radio for information and adventure. There was always time in the afternoon for a half hour of Tom Mix or the Lone Ranger on the radio. If you have trouble with this concept think of it in terms of the person who reads a book versus the person who sees the movie version of the same story.

Eddie is not a hero. He does not come from a privileged family or even one that is moderately well off. He is average in every sense. He is like millions of other middle-class kids who grew up in the Mid-West in the 1900s. He succeeds in spite of the struggles of that time of our history and has fun doing it all. Life was good but hard during those times but people persevered nonetheless; and they enjoyed that life. Things were simpler then and moved at a slower pace. Families were closer. People were trusted. Doors were left unlocked as were cars. Kids were allowed to roam unaccompanied anywhere in their area. Money was dear and valued much more than now. Hobos roamed the United States and were given chores to do by the populace in return for a meal and even sometimes a bed. Today they are called "homeless" and discarded or shunned as if they are not human beings like the rest of us.

Today Eddie would be called a tree-hugger and looked down on because he does not enjoy inflicting pain on animals as in hunting. Eddie hunted when he was young but didn't really enjoy the kill as he was "supposed" to do. Instead he would stand over the sad, lifeless body of an otherwise beautiful wild animal and privately grieve about the death of that child of God. Still, he could become a very effective hunter of humans in later life as a Naval Aviator.

Eddie is as complicated as any other human. The following pages attempt to portray a middle-class kid as he grows up. Everything in the book is true to life. The author makes no apologies for anything written about the youngster. It happened as it happened. The reader is free to draw their own conclusions about the kid as he grows into an adult.

Edward Landers

Acknowledgements

It has become the custom of writers to publish some sort of acknowledgement concerning things such as what drove him to write whatever he has written, the people who have helped and aided him along the way and various other people who are simply notables in the author's mind and therefore somehow need to be mentioned if, for no other reason, so that they might see their names in print. I offer the following in pursuit of the truth.

I am, at various times, a cynic, a pragmatist, a Tatar and a benevolent person depending on the time and place. I do not suffer fools lightly and have no use for elitists or bullies. Please keep these attributes in mind as you read my acknowledgements.

First of all, I wish to acknowledge and thank the uneducated and under educated black kids that I encountered daily in junior high school. Their use of what they believed was the English language imbued me with a longing to learn what the language was really all about in an effort to avoid sounding like them. Much later a very ignorant lecturer at a minor California college would call such drivel "Ebonics". I did not wish to become associated in any way with such propaganda directed at the uneducated among us. I shudder whenever I hear what passes for speech when the speaker uses such cacophony and I deplore the use of words and phrases of that type of noise into the English language.

Secondly I would like to give special credit to those very religious people who are more hypocritical than truly religious. You know the kind; the righteous people who parade about prattling about their purity and pretending to point out the faults of others. As I recall Jesus was reported to address this kind of person when he cautioned the concern with the "mote in your brother's eye" while ignoring the "beam in your own eye". They taught me more than anyone can really measure although not the type of learning they probably would have wished. They imbued in me the absolute urge to not follow in their footsteps.

Then there are the bullies or the would-be bullies among us. I have made it a lifelong task to ferret out people like that and make their life as hard as possible in a desperate effort to re-educate them and turn them into productive people instead of savages.

Special thanks should also go to the elitist among us. As I observed them in the growing-up process I intuitively knew that I did not wish to become anything like them. As the old saying goes, "they only bother you if you listen to them".

I would like to thank the teachers in my high school with special thanks to those who taught the science classes. They were universally excellent although seriously underpaid. They filled up my empty glass of knowledge and left me with a life-long thirst for truth.

The Salvation Army and the United States Navy have to figure in here somewhere. Without those two groups I would be only a wandering soul looking for fulfillment in obscure places.

I'm sure that I could continue this line of thought but the reader probably would become quickly bored and I'm sure that, by this time, I have made my points. Please refer to this article if you have any questions about my conduct or thought processes as you read.

Edward Landers

Chapter One

Where to begin? The further back I reach into the swirling mists of time the harder it is to differentiate between my own memories and those things that were related to me by my mother. Generally my own memories are vague feelings and impressions. Related stories, coming to me much later are clearer in my mind.

My first memories are of my mother's body. I took much comfort from resting on her lap with my head cradled against her bosom. It was confusing sometime later when I was prohibited from fondling her breasts. Apparently she felt uneasy when I did so but how do you explain that to a very young boy? Lectures about the birds and bees would come years later if at all.

For some unexplained reason I felt an affinity with large female breasts. I took comfort not only in my mother's breasts but in those of other ladies as well. Most of the females I groped seemed to be very amused at my actions, perhaps because of my very young age. I learned a little later that interdictions of that type were promptly discouraged.

I was born on the 27th day of January in 1936 in Terre Haute, Indiana. The town is located in the southern part of Indiana, not far from the Kentucky state line. Terre Haute means "high ground" in Latin. The town is situated on the banks of the Wabash River. Winters in southern Indiana are generally mild but in any case the weather wasn't much of a problem because I was born at home. People in those days didn't go to a hospital unless they were in immanent danger of dying and childbirth was considered much the same as a toothache in the relative order of things, at least by the men folk of that era.

I don't recall too much of my early childhood in Indiana but my mother said that I seemed inordinately afraid of being run over by a car. Probably a good thing as we lived on a busy street in town and children, once they were able to walk, were left to their own devices. I can remember a family grieving over a child who had been overrun by a car. They were devastated, as one can imagine, and the street was covered with blood and gore from their son. I came on the scene as the result of following all of the sirens and was shocked at witnessing the gore in the street. I'll never forget the sight of the child's mother who stood on the curb and sobbed, comforted only by her husband. The family was black (actually the mother and father were a pleasing shade of brown, not that it mattered especially) so not much was made of the accident other than to promptly hose off the area so as to not annoy the people who had to drive by. I was struck, even at that early age, of the casual treatment of the whole episode. It was business as usual. There were no psychologists to counsel the parents or anyone else who happened to witness the morbid situation. That would come many years later as the psychology people became more numerous and were able to form a sort of lobby in their attempts to gain recognition. Perhaps that was why I was so worried about cars and how they might impact me.

All of my grandparents lived in Terre Haute at the time. My maternal grandmother lived in town in a nice brick home with my unmarried aunt and her second husband, George. My grandfather had died from tuberculosis when my mother was a little girl. Grandfather had worked a small subsistance farm near Farmers City, Illinois. I have a picture of him sitting in an old rocking chair outside of their house. The chair sits on dirt underneath a dead tree. There is not a blade of grass in sight. It is a poignant picture of stark reality and poverty. When Grandfather died his family moved to Terre Haute, Indiana.

George worked at the Champaign Velvet brewery in Terre Haute and was an alcoholic before the word existed for the general population. He used to walk two miles to work each day and would carry home a full case of beer each evening, which he would consume that night, only to carry the empty case of bottles back to the brewery the next day to be refilled. George Issler was as German as they came. He carefully coached me how to spell his name and when I could successfully do so he gave me a whole dollar. It was a fortune and it was silver and not paper.

George also taught me a little song that I've never forgotten. It went thus:

> An old Heine vun night,
> He got very tight.
> He valked into a shaloon,
> Und started to fight.
> He got hit in der head,
> Mit a bucket uff beer,
> Und died mit a viener,
> Vass shtuck in hiss ear.

George was very proud of being able to teach me that little ditty. Obviously it has remained with me to this day.

Aunt Bernice was what some folks unkindly called an old maid. She was deformed from birth with a concave chest and a face that "took a little getting used to" but possessed a good mind and a beautiful disposition. My mother used to beat up the kids in school who made fun of her sister.

My maternal grandmother was a feisty, little woman. When I say she was "little" it was in the sense that she was short but 'hefty". She was a Scots-Irish, no-nonsense farm woman who took no hostages. I can remember that she would become angry with her husband for some infraction and, at times like that, she would carry a razor strop (a heavy piece of leather) and would administer justice with it over George's back liberally any time she happened to encounter him. George tried very hard to elude her but was generally unsuccessful and the razor strop made contact a lot, convincing George that Grandma was the top dog in that family.

Mom used to tell me about the time that Grandma couldn't sleep because a cat was sitting on a fence in her back yard on the farm caterwauling and generally making a lot of noise. Mom said that Grandma took her .22 caliber rifle and potted the poor cat squarely in the head thereby solving the problem at least as far as Grandma was concerned. My Grandma was obviousely an Annie Oakley. My Mother's brother inherited that rifle and today his son, my cousin, owns it.

My paternal grandparents lived on a very nice farm in Terre Haute. There were five children in the family, my father being the oldest. The four younger kids lived at home on the farm. My grandmother was a small, saintly woman. She put up with my curmudgeon grandfather who used his children to run the farm while he attended to his own insurance company. He was generally disliked by everyone and his own family was no exception to this general preference. He enforced discipline in his family with his leather belt. His wife was not excluded in this regard. I was young but not entirely stupid and I can distinctly remember the stories about my grandfather; about how he would beat his children with the leather belt even after they had fallen on the floor. As most kids were prone to do at that time they would gripe among themselves but thoughts of mutiny were nonexistent. Memories remained long after the incidents, however, and emerged full-blown later on.

My grandparent's farm was a working farm complete with a cow and some chickens. I always enjoyed the task of milking the cow, especially when my uncles would hold one of the several cats that lived on the farm on their knees and squirt milk into the open mouths of the kitties directly from the cow's teats. I didn't care for the onerous task of harvesting a chicken for the family's dinner. My uncles didn't care for it much either but as good farm kids they completed their tasks without complaint. The sight of a headless chicken flopping in the yard and spraying blood all over the place didn't do much for my peace of mind. There were several methods of dispatching the unlucky chicken that had been chosen for the ultimate sacrifice. One uncle adopted the method of grabbing the chicken by its head and neck and swinging it around in a circle until the head separated from the body. Another method involved placing a board on the unhappy chicken's neck and pulling the body until it separated from the head. A third uncle chose only to shoot the bird with his .22 caliber rifle. I personally thought that this was the best way. It separated the dispatcher from the dispatched, was clean as compared to the "wet" method as defined by later military standards and may have figured into my later-in-life choice of becoming a pilot instead of a "grunt". You see, pilots are able to kill efficiently and with impunity, never having to see the results of their actions.

I had a friend who lived a few doors away from our home in Terre Haute. I can distinctly remember that his house had no indoor plumbing and had an outhouse. The back yard had no grass and was a mass of dirt and clay. My friend's mother used to empty the dish washing water by throwing it onto the back yard. We never played in his back yard as it always smelled of washing soap.

Very early in my childhood we moved to Kansas City, Missouri. My father was employed by a local dairy delivering milk to houses and businesses along an established route. It must have been a colorful route as he used to tell of delivering to whore houses where he was invited in to have coffee with the ladies who worked and resided there. Apparently they were adept at not mixing business and pleasure as nothing ever came of his coffee klatches and my mother ignored the whole business. The milk route was in a run-down part of the city where simply walking around invited mayhem. My father gloried in his exciting new job. It gave him a copious amount of material to talk about and talk about it he did. A few restaurants were on his milk route. He used to relate that he was apprehensive of the Chinese cooks who worked in the kitchens of those restaurants. One day he thought that he was in danger. The cooks were gathered in a circle chattering loudly in Chinese while shaking meat cleavers and sharp knives at each other. As he watched, wondering if he should flee or not all of a sudden heads were thrown back in loud laughter. They had been telling jokes. Kansas City was the home of a political machine run by a gentleman called Pendergas. Apparently he was not a very nice man as my father used to fight against him in an effort to overthrow his political regime. My father had some very exciting stories to tell about physical fights involving gangs of men, of shootings and underhanded dealings. At least they were exciting to a young boy and the lessons learned were those of not bending to the will of a draconian political boss. I was honored one evening by being allowed to attend a political rally with my parents. During the rally a dissident started shouting and disrupted the proceedings. The police collared him and removed him from the auditorium. Shortly thereafter there was the sound of a gunshot. My Dad looked at my Mom and said, "I guess they shot him." Nothing else came of the incident.

We lived in a hotel in Kansas City. Now that I am older I can hardly believe that a young family would choose to live in a hotel on a more or less permanent basis but apparently housing was hard to come by and hotels were cheaper then than they are today. I have a few actual memories of this period, mostly centered on several traumatic occurrences that happened during this time. One of these memories is of the time I fell off of a couch where I was sleeping onto a fleet of little cars I had been playing with and which were laying on the floor.

In 1938 it was common for some cars to be outfitted with large advertising signs that were attached to the roof of the car. The signs were aligned longitudinally on the car and jutted up to four feet into the air. Several businesses advertised in this manner, one of which was the Roi-Tan Cigar Company. My parents had given me several toy cars that were miniatures of the Roi-Tan cars and were made of real metal. Plastics were generally unknown at that time. When I fell off of the couch I fell onto one of the signs, which cut my lip like a knife. I remember my panicked mother taking me to the local pharmacy where the pharmacist stopped the bleeding and bandaged me. People of that time rarely sought the services of a real doctor. That was reserved for really serious things like amputations. I can still remember the smell of the pharmacy. That smell I now know was the odor of Tincture of Benzoin. I've always thought of it as a pleasant smell. I still have that scar on my upper lip.

I also remember getting my arm stuck between the coils of a steam radiator that served to heat our apartment in the winter. I had been looking out of the window at the Christmas lights and my arm slid into the radiator when I lost my balance. My mother was panicked once again as she couldn't dislodge my arm and I was, of course, screaming as the radiator was hot and was burning my arm. I can remember the discussions among neighbors who counseled calling the local fire fighters. Some cool headed person finally dislodged the arm, which was not all that burned and things settled down once more. Whenever I was sick my folks usually took me to the resident pharmacist who ran a small drug store in the hotel. The pharmacist could usually come up with some remedy that seemed to work thus saving the family an expensive trip to a real doctor. That was the normal method of handling injuries or sicknesses back then. I don't think that I suffered from the lack of frequent trips to a doctor as children are subjected to today.

We spent a couple of years in Kansas City and then moved back to Terre Haute, Indiana once more. My awareness was a little more acute now and I remember ash pits in the alleys where the ashes from the coal furnaces were dumped, to be collected by the trash collectors later in the week. I will never forget the acrid smell of anthracite coal ashes. Snowplows were unheard of in cities and towns being reserved for highways, and the ashes were used to keep cars from slipping and skidding on the roads. Ashes were everywhere especially in the alleys, which were ubiquitous. Cautious drivers would attach chains on their tires in order to obtain traction but chains cost money, which was in relative short supply in the thirties. Most people counted on the local populace dumping their ashes on the roads and alleys in order to keep cars from sliding around. Needless to say, by the springtime the roads were slightly messy but that was just considered the price of doing things in that era.

That was in the winter. In the summer I remember the Iceman. He drove a horse drawn cart containing large blocks of ice that were delivered to each house that displayed a square sign in a window requesting ice. The sign was simple. It consisted of four triangles joined at the apices so as to form a square when joined. Each triangle boasted a number signifying the amount of ice requested by the homeowner, 25, 50, 75, and 100 pounds. The iceman would halt his patient horse, climb up into his cart, use his ice pick to chip off the required block of ice, hoist it onto his back, which he protected with a large piece of leather, walk to the house, knock on the door and place the block of ice into the ice chest that served as an ice box for the household. The homeowner would open the front door for the iceman and allow him to walk through the home, open up the ice chest and place the ice block in it. Electric refrigerators were generally an unknown item. The Iceman's name was Carl. I never knew his last name; Carl was the only name anyone ever called him. Carl was always followed by small groups of children who delighted in climbing on his cart when he was delivering ice and stealing small chunks of ice to be consumed during the hot weather. It was heady excitement for the kids who thought that they were doing something slightly against some law by "stealing" the little shards of ice left by Carl. Carl never seemed to mind the kids. He mostly ignored them even when they got in his way by trying to pet his horse. Both Carl and his horse were quiet, stoic, solid, unassuming citizens. They belonged to a different time period when things were slower and people took their time doing most things. The kids all pretended to be afraid of Carl but that man was a paragon of gentleness and caring. He cared for his horse, his customers and the kids, in that order. Sometimes, when his ice pick had not chipped off enough ice slivers to satisfy the clamoring kids surrounding his wagon I've seen Carl chip a little extra off of the large ice blocks so that even the littlest kid could steal some ice from his wagon as he made his delivery. The ice had been cut from the local river in the wintertime, placed in an icehouse and covered with sawdust from the local sawmill in order to insulate it from the summer sun. The system worked well enough, did not require any electricity, employed both humans and horses and furnished throngs of kids with pleasure of an innocent type.

Today the thought of children eating ice that had come from the river would send chills up every parent's spine. The FDA, the USDA and a myriad of other government agencies would be upset and the ice company would probably be sued and forced to shut down. To my knowledge no child ever got sick from eating the little pieces of ice they had managed to "steal" from Carl's wagon.

The icebox that served as a refrigerator in those days used only ice to cool the food that was kept inside. The ice would, of course, melt as time went on. The water that resulted from the melt would drip into the drip pan underneath the icebox. If the pan was not emptied it would overflow and make a mess of the floor. It was my job to empty the pan twice a day.

Ice for the icebox was not expensive but it did require a certain amount of money. My family never had much money so we cut corners whenever and wherever we could. In the winter Dad used to cancel the services of the iceman. Dad would obtain an empty orange crate, which was, at that time, made of wood, and would attach it to the kitchen window so that we could place any food items requiring cooling in the crate simply by opening the window. The winter temperatures were sufficient to effectively replace the ice that Carl furnished.

Dad had a job driving a truck for a local short haul company. The trucks were not well maintained but a job was a job and the pay was steady. One day Dad was driving down a hill in the rolling countryside around Vincennes, Indiana when the truck's brakes failed. He ended up crashing the whole rig in a culvert at the foot of the hill as he couldn't make the turn because of the speed build-up. The trailer became uncoupled from the cab and flattened the cab against the bank of the culvert. Luckily Dad was thrown from the cab (seat belts had not been thought of back then) and ended up in the ditch as the cab was flattened. His only injury was to his knee. He was taken to a local hospital where a surgeon removed a lot of the cartilage and fat that cushions the knee joint. Dad never regained full use of that leg and used a cane for years after that.

Mom and dad were young folks and, as many young people tend to be, were slightly wild and fun loving. Mom took up smoking at an early age and never gave that habit up until much later in life when she developed tuberculosis. I can remember one evening a bunch of friends and my parents were going to a night club. The car was full so Mom rode on the outside on the running board holding on to the window sill. She lost her purse on a curve and everyone had to hunt for it along the highway in the dark.

Running Boards—Cars today do not have these niceties that made entering the car easily. They generally ran from the front to the rear fenders and were wide enough to enable anyone to stand on them and to hold onto the car comfortably while it was moving.

Mosquitoes were a perennial problem in Terre Haute. My mother used to ask the local grocer for the banana stalk after all of the bananas had been cut off of it and sold. Bananas used to be delivered to stores on the stalk and not packaged neatly as they are today. Apparently the old wives tales held that a banana stalk would keep mosquitoes away. I used to listen to the radio a lot (there was no television) and I had heard that mosquitoes needed still water in order to reproduce. We had an old cistern in the back yard that was replenished by rain water. It was covered by a cement cap but had a large hole in the middle of the cap where a pump used to be housed in order to raise the cistern water that was used for bathing and washing hair and clothing. The cistern wasn't used any more but it was an ideal place for mosquito breeding. I got a quart of old engine oil from my father and poured it into the cistern. That stopped most of the mosquitoes. Mom would never believe the "old wives' tale" that held the idea that mosquitoes were hatched in old cisterns but the idea worked at any rate.

Mom always got her banana stalks from a local grocer, an old German named Oding. That was his last name and most housewives only called him by that name. There were, of course, "supermarkets" like the Great Alantic and Pacific Tea Company, called the "A and P", but they were much smaller than the supermarkets of today and necessitated the use of a car to travel to them. Grandma Issler used to use the family car to go to the A and P once every two weeks. Most housewives used the tiny corner grocery stores almost excusively.

Oding weighed the cuts of meat he sold to the public with an old scale mounted on top of the meat counter where everyone could readily read the weight. The old scale would bounce a little when anything was placed on it and, at busy times, Oding would try to steady the scale by placing a finger on it. Of course some housewives thought that Oding was cheating by adding a little weight to the final tab. I can remember several times that someone would scream at him and tell him to get his finger off the scale. Oding was implacable and would only answer, "Jah, jah, jah".

When I got old enough to run errands to the little grocery store Mom would occasionally give me a written note to give to Oding along with some money to pay for the purchase. I was always proud to be allowed to go to the store for her and felt quite grown up in doing so. It was always a mystery as the purchase was wrapped tightly in a plain brown paper wrapping. One day I asked Oding what was in the bag. He turned red in the face and said, "You got to ask your Mom". I did so and she told me that it was none of my business. The mystery continued until much later when I found out that the mysterious package contained a feminine product called Kotex. We weren't all that removed from the Victorian age.

One day as I was walking along a sidewalk near our home I passed a shrub that emitted a strange hissing or rustling sound. Curiosity got the best of me and, after parting the leaves I found a female bat with two infant bats attached to her teats. She was protecting them from harm by spreading her wings and hissing. I was fascinated. I watched the little bat for some time until finally an adult interferred, wondering what I was doing. When I pointed out the tiny family he reacted violently. He found a club and killed all three of the little animals while I watched, horrified. I couldn't believe that anyone would kill a tiny animal that was no threat to anyone and was only trying to protect her young. The image of that has always stayed in my mind.

Sometime around 1940 we moved to Santa Anna, California. I was never consulted about that move but I've heard that it was accomplished in order for my father to find a better job. He had no skills and menial labor in Terre Haute revolved around working at the local brewery. Initially we lived in a small rented house in Santa Anna with a fenced in back yard. I was supposed to stay inside the yard, as there was a busy street nearby. Being possessed of an independent mind I strayed outside of the protective yard often.

I didn't know it but cars weren't the only danger outside of the yard. Each day a "big" boy would walk by our house. I only categorized him as a "big" boy as he acted more like a boy than an adult, however he was fully grown. He had long hair and was generally disheveled. He constantly sang a song that was current at that time that ran, "South of the border, down Mexico way." I called him "South of the Border." He would always stop and talk to me asking me if I wouldn't come outside of the yard. Both of my parents were aware of him, as I had talked about him at length. He was fascinating. No other adult would even notice let alone talk to me. I was flattered. My parents had warned me to avoid him and to not talk to him but I ignored their advice. I was adept at ignoring my parent's advice.

One day as I was playing outside the yard, "South of the Border" happened by. He stopped and talked to me as usual. All of a sudden he grabbed me and stuck his hand down my pants. He grabbed my penis and produced a very large pocketknife. "How'd ya like me to cut your cock off?" he said. I didn't really know just what a cock was as that was another word I had never heard but I got the idea. I pleaded with him not to do anything with the knife and apparently that satisfied him as he grinned, put the knife back in his pocket and left me feeling shaken and vulnerable.

When I told my parents about the incident I fully expected to be punished for what I considered to be an infraction. They were very alarmed and my father made several dire threats about what he intended to do to "South of the Border." The man never appeared again although my father watched intently for him to do so. In retrospect the police were never consulted about the incident. In the 1940s people tended to take care of themselves and their families on their own. The police were there for "maintaining the peace". How different it is today when every citizen thinks that the police are there to "protect them" and no one makes any effort to take care of themselves or to protect themselves. Police are generally "historians" and usually are around to take statements and investigate any crime that has already been accomplished.

My father decided that I needed a dog for company. I concurred. What little boy can resist a dog? My family finally settled on a small rat terrier we named Toy. Toy was a very nice dog and was lots of company but a small child isn't really constituted to handle a small dog let alone a small terrier. I was abusive to the dog who had a mind of his own and rarely obeyed. We were two of a kind since I rarely obeyed also. What could anyone expect? Toy was a Terrier. Terriers have a mind of their own. That's what endears them to their owners. My father would patiently try and teach me how to handle the little dog gently but I remained too rough for him. Finally my father, in desperation, told me that everything I did to the dog that was unkind he would do to me. I tested the water, of course. When I would make the dog lie on the ground in order to use him for a pillow, my father would make me lay down and he would use me for a pillow. When I threw dirt on the dog my dad did the same to me. One day I kicked the dog and my dad made me assume the position of all fours while he gently kicked me. Apparently I had had enough of this nonsense. Now I don't remember this part at all but I'm reliably informed that one day I urinated on the dog while my father watched in horror. He says that I then told him, "Just let me see you do that to me." I don't know the outcome of that episode but Toy shortly disappeared and my father reverted to corporeal punishment in a futile attempt to enforce discipline.

My Dad finally became a bus driver for the Bay City Transit Company in Santa Monica, California. We rented an apartment near the beach initially. There was an absolute lack of grass around the apartment but as much sand as a young boy could ever wish for. I could dig anywhere and make as many sand castles as I wished. I could never figure out just what the semi hard pieces of sand were that I used to dig up. They were very curious. I finally gave up trying to solve the puzzle and would simply discard them as I couldn't find any use for them. I completely discounted the existence of the numerous cats that prowled the area that considered the whole world to be their toilet.

There were quite a few other kids who lived in the area so I never lacked for playmates. Little boys can become very busy in their playing and sometimes are much too busy to come inside in order to urinate. I adopted the habit of using any bush as a urinal much to the distress of my parents. Lectures were of no avail in stopping this habit, as I was rather stubborn even at that early age. Finally my father thought to solve the problem by a rather unique method. He would make me pull down my short pants, produce my bare penis, which he would coat with rubbing alcohol and then would lock me in a closet. In later years having studied some psychology I was amused at the memory. Any psychologist would have had a field day at the implications from that odd practice. I would roar at being insulted by having my penis assaulted by rubbing alcohol but my thought was that my father must have thought that the incident would cause pain. I was used to pain as I was a healthy, normal boy and thus incurred my share of spankings. It was my firm belief that if I did not show that I was being pained the punishment would increase until the punisher could see that he was having the desired effect. Therefore, it was impingent upon me to cry, bawl, roar or in anyway show that I was being tortured satisfactorily. Making a lot of noise when my penis was being coated with alcohol insured that real pain would not be meted out, or so I thought. It didn't hurt at all. Locking me in a dark closet, contrary to what current psychology would have you think, didn't affect me at all. It was quiet, dark, warm and comforting with all of the familiar clothing and smells. I could relax and even find cracks whereby I could spy on my antagonists. The downside was that I missed out on playtime. The practice did nothing to discourage me from peeing on the bushes in the neighborhood but did make me plan to find more private bushes that were hidden from my parents. I never did find out just what my father intended or what he thought that he was accomplishing by coating my penis with alcohol. It had absolutely no effect on me but in the current era it would most certainly have placed my father under the scrutiny of the law and probably have subjected him to a court proceeding. None of this has ever had any effect on the course of history or the price of bread. One has to wonder why all of the fuss.

I turned five years of age while we lived in this place. It was 1941 and there was a war in Europe. I knew nothing about a war, of course, but it bothered me that my parents were so involved in reading the news that they had little time for me. I couldn't understand just what the news was but I knew that it was important to my folks.

One day my mother asked me if I wanted to take a walk with her and see one of my friends who had started school. I missed his company and was eager to see him so I readily agreed. We walked to a local school where my mother introduced me to a teacher. She taught kindergarten. I played in the schoolyard with my friend for a short time and then my mother asked me if I wanted to stay with him for a while. I readily agreed and she left. In a very short time the teacher called all of the kids inside. I was ready to go home but she informed me that I could not do so. It was then that I learned that you couldn't trust your parents. My own mother had sold me into slavery. I was a prisoner. I had to do what some complete stranger wanted me to do and none of the other kids even cared that we were all prisoners. They even seemed to enjoy the incarceration. I can remember that I felt like crying but I sucked it up as best I could since "big boys did not cry".

Eventually I got used to school and learned to enjoy it like the other kids did. I was used to discipline and quickly buckled down to the learning process. Later in life when I contemplated this I would point to it humerously as "The Stockholm syndrome" or "Brainwashing". We used to have what was called then as "quiet time". Quiet time was accomplished by adjusting your body on a straight board furnished for that purpose in either the supine or the prone position. At least we were allowed that choice. The boards were always stacked at the back of the classroom. They were approximately the size of a single bed mattress and had small feet attached in order to keep the kids off of the floor. When "quiet time" was announced all of the kids would file to the back of the room, chose a board and carry it to any acceptable spot in the room where they were required to lie down. There were no covers or pillows, just boards. There was always some competition as to just where to place the boards. Clicks were rampant and the space around the click leader was always jealously guarded. I was always a loner and therefore never was allowed access to any of the clicks of kids. My quiet time was always spent alone, quietly and thoughtfully thinking about my lot in life.

Later on in school "quiet time" was not called by that name but was quiet time, nevertheless. Students were required not to lie on boards but were required to set quietly in their seats with their hands exhibited prominently on the desk in front of them. The edict of having to place your hands on the desk at all times was uncomfortable but satisfied the teacher. Apparently she figured that if a child, especially a boy, was allowed free use of their hands nothing but mischief would occur. There was absolutely no talking, reading, writing or coloring. You couldn't even pick your nose. I soon figured out that quiet time was for the purpose of allowing the teachers some time for themselves and had nothing at all to do with the psyche of the students.

Much later in life I heard of the saying, "Children should be seen and not heard". All of the teachers I had in grade school adhered faithfully to that saying. I can never remember any time that I was allowed to speak out freely or even talk to other students most of the time except at recess. The older I became and the higher in the system I got the more stringent the rule. "Thou shalt not talk." Forget the First Amendment to the Constitution. Free speech was proscribed. Maybe that's why Constitutional law isn't taught until much later in life.

My family saved most of my early "report cards" and one in particular always made me laugh when I had occasion to read it. The teacher who had issued the card had a problem with me as I was apparently very talkative. She had written, "Eddie needs to be more attentive to the rules. When the bell rings it means "quiet please" but Eddie just keeps on talking and playing." I could picture an indignant older lady with pursed lips writing her complaints on my report card.

I was taught not only by the teachers but also by the students. One day another boy asked me, "Have you ever seen a nigger?" I had no idea what he was talking about, as I had never heard the word used before. I answered truthfully, "No". He said, "C'mon, I'll show you one."

I followed him to the swings in the playground. He pointed out a small black boy in one of the swings saying, "That's a nigger." I was always a friendly boy so as soon as the other boy vacated the swing I walked up to him and said, "Hi, nigger."

I may not have known the meaning of the word but he obviously did. He hit me squarely on my nose knocking me into the dirt. As I sat there stunned and bleeding he walked off without even saying a word. It was a valuable but painful lesson that I've never forgotten.

In December of 1941 the empire of Japan decided to attack Pearl Harbor participating us into war in the Pacific. Every student in the school was issued a "dog tag" that documented their names, addresses and any other item of interest needed. Most kids got the free tags that looked like the tags that the military wore. My parents thought that they were too large and so they took me to a local jeweler and had a smaller, round tag cut for me. I was ashamed of my tag as it didn't look like the ones the other kids wore but I was stuck with the small tag anyway.

We had to practice air raid drills in school. Everyone had to crawl under their desks during the drills and we were drilled in the "alert" and the "all clear" signals. I always thought that the kids in the upper grades had the most fun during any of the drills as they could jump into the large fire escape tube on the top floors of the school and slide around in the spiral interior slide to shoot out the bottom. Those fire escapes looked like fearsome apparitions but I thought that it would be wonderful if I could only try it one time.

It didn't seem fair to me but then everything seemed unfair to a young kid in the 40s. No one paid attention in the least to a kid. On the other hand we were allowed a lot of freedom back then. I used to get an allowance, even in kindergarten and the first grade, of 25 cents a week. It was a fortune. I could do anything I wished with it. My parents let me walk all the way to the amusement pier on the beach in Santa Monica. I was allowed to wander around as much as I wanted to wander. I could go to the movie (there was only one) or squander my fortune on the amusement machines that abounded on the pier. The only requirement for me to observe was that I had to be home before dark. I marvel on the freedom that I had then. Today if your child is missing for even a few minutes panic usually ensues. When I was four or five years old my mom didn't worry about me until the sun had set. I was free to wander anywhere I wished.

I remember the cigarettes called "Wings". The packages always had a card that had a picture of one of the military airplanes the United States had in its inventory. Of course I didn't smoke but both of my parents did. Just about all adults did. I used to collect the cards from my parents and their friends would save their cards for me. The wonderful cards with the wonderful pictures of airplanes made good trading materiel for kids.

I can also remember a few light-hearted and catchy songs that were simply fun and without much meaning but they were very popular and everyone sang them. One of them was called "Mairzy doats". It went something like this:

"Mairzy doats and dozy doats and liddle lamzy divy. A Kiddley divey too, wouldn't chew?"

The song went on to say. "If the words sound queer and funny to your ear, a little bit jumbled and jivey. Sing Mares eat oats and does eat oats and little lambs eat ivy. A kid'll eat ivy too, wouldn't you?"

Another one was, "Down in the meadow in a little bitty pool, Swam three little fishies and a Momma fishie too, 'Swim' said the mamma fishie, 'swim if you can' and they swam and they swam all over the dam. Boop boop dittem dattem wattam chew" . . . . and it went on and on but you get the picture.

Then there was the "Hut-sut" song about a Swedish boy. The chorus went, "Hut sut rawlson on the rillerah and a brawla brawla sooit" and was repeated a number of times.

The words might have been silly but the tunes were catchy and were far nicer to listen to than the current "rap" cacaphony.

I had few worries in those halcyon days. The only thing I really worried about were the very few bullies that inevitably cropped up now and then. I was ever on the alert for them. Bullies, I found, were a way of life for any group of kids anywhere. I'm sure that kids in

Afghanistan or South Africa or China have the same concerns. Adults didn't scare me a bit but the testosterone driven, early maturing kid my own age scared the daylights out of me. They were unpredictable, you see. You never knew if they wanted to befriend you or knock the daylights out of you. It all depended on their mood and they were always moody. It was easier to avoid them completely.

I used to keep a weather eye out for any kid my age that suddenly appeared several blocks ahead of me. Whenever I spotted an unfamiliar one I would cross the street immediately. If he crossed the street also I could be reasonably sure that he probably wished to confront me. In that case I turned tail and left the field of battle. It worked most of the time. I became adept at finding new ways of getting home. I wasn't always successful, of course, and several times I reported home bawling and scuffed from a battle that I never seemed to win. I wasn't much of a fighter. Early on, my Dad attempted to teach me how to box. He tied boxing gloves on me, donned them himself and we squared off. The first time he hit me I gave up. It hurt! Instead of trying to encourage me he made fun of me, calling me a sissy. That was OK with me. I would rather be a sissy than to be pummeled. I would much rather win my battles with my brain than my chin.

One such bully lived right across the street. I can still remember his name. Bobby. Sometimes he delighted in playing soldier or cops and robbers with me but other times he delighted in pounding my head into the dirt. I used to enter the house bawling in pain and embarrassment. My mother would commiserate with me and counsel me to "not play with Bobby any more". Fat chance. Have you ever tried to shun a bully who lives right across the street from you?

My father was a lot more direct in his counseling sessions. One day I reported for duty, scuffed, dirty, snot-nosed and bawling. My father asked me what had happened. I told him. He said, "Eddie, you need to hit him harder than he hits you. If you come into this house crying again I'll give you a spanking." I was much more afraid of my father than I was of Bobby. I sobered up and gave my dilemma a lot of thought.

My father unknowingly had adopted the techniques that the U.S. Marine Corps used. Much later in life I asked my wife why she thought that Marines would charge straight up a hill in the face of withering machine gun fire. When she professed ignorance I supplied the answer. "Those Marines are more afraid of the Sergeant leading them than they are of the hostiles shooting at them".

The next time Bobby decided to chastise me I picked up a handy tree limb that had advantageously fallen near me and walloped him over the head with it. I didn't want him to get mad at me and take the limb away only to use it against me so I kept hitting him as he howled for mercy. He finally ran off to tell his parents about the bully across the street. Boy! Was I proud of myself!

In a short while Bobby's father showed up on our front porch with a complaint. My father answered the door and listened carefully to the complaining adult while I eavesdropped in another room. My father finally said, "I'll take care of the problem. It won't happen again." Bobby's dad left in a huff and I stood to for the inevitable punishment. Heretofore I had always been counseled to be peaceful and never to start any trouble. My father looked around and found me lurking around a corner. "Nice job", he said, "I'm proud of you. I don't think Bobby will try and beat up on you again."

And he never did. I was so proud of myself that I thought my shirt buttons would pop off. Not only had I vanquished a formidable foe but my father, who was sparing in his praise, had actually given me a complement. All was right in the world.

I had an insatiable curiosity as a young boy. In reality that curiosity has never diminished, luckily, as I deem curiosity to be one of the most valuable attributes a person can possess. I used to prowl the back alleys rummaging into the trash of all of our neighbors. It was wonderful what treasures a small boy could find in the trash. One of the best finds was always an old clock. You could keep busy for days taking an old clock apart and each screw that was removed produced other smaller treasures in the form of tiny cogs and wheels. Since all of the trash was relegated to alleys there was no stigma attached to a family possessing a trash rummager as he was generally hidden from the public view. My father laughingly referred to me as "garbage-can Joe". I didn't care. He had no idea what wonderful things one could find in the back alleys. An added perk was that the alleys contained very few bullies looking for prey.

One day a special person arrived at our front door. He had a telegram for my father. My father's brother, Paul, had been killed in an aircraft accident in a strange place called Naval Air Station, Great Lakes, Illinois. My father was decimated. My mother told me that I had lost an uncle but I had never met him so I was unaffected. Not so my father. He mourned for a few days and finally announced that he was going to enlist in the Navy and kill Japs. My mother attempted to reason with him but the next day he left to enlist. He returned home the same day with the news that he was 4F, whatever that meant. Much earlier in my short life he had been employed as a truck driver in Indiana and had been in an accident with a truck that had faulty breaks. The pile of metal that remained of the truck was spectacular and the only thing that saved my father was the fact that he had been thrown clear of the wreckage before the trailer that had become uncoupled from the cab had pancaked it. He did incur a torn knee that had to be rebuilt. The knee was the fly in the ointment and the US Navy did not want a gimpy sailor.

Not to be discouraged my father then became an Air Raid Warden. For those of you who do not know what an air raid is, it is an attack on native soil by enemy airplanes that intend on bombing and strafing (firing at the ground and anything on it by the plane's guns and cannon). He was trained in first aid procedures and police techniques. It was his job during an air raid to roam the neighborhood making sure that windows showed no lights that could become targets for planes dropping bombs. I was very proud of him in his uniform and he took me on several trips to show me the smudge pots that he had to ignite that would throw up a smoke screen to confuse the attacking planes. We also inspected the barrage balloons that he would release in case of an attack. The balloons were tethered and had a myriad of wires below them that an aircraft would become entangled with if they flew low enough to fire their guns. If they flew into the balloon itself the balloon would explode. It was a very exciting time for a young boy.

One day my father took me to the beach to see an airplane that had ditched offshore and was being recovered. It was a P-38 and was the most beautiful airplane I had ever seen or ever would see. I later learned that the Japanese pilots called it "the forked tailed devil" but it was beautiful from my point of view. A man tried to take a picture of the plane and a military policeman took his camera away from him and destroyed it. A few days later a Japanese submarine surfaced offshore and shelled a few oil wells. At least everyone thought that it was a Japanese submarine. That seemed to make sense since we were supposed to be at war with them.

The current word among the residents in California was that the "Japs" were all against the United States. Most of them were being rounded up and sent some place else. Those that were left still stoically worked their remarkable farms. What else could they do? Where could they go? Mom used to say that it was a shame that she had to strip off so many leaves from the lettuce heads that she bought on the open market because "the Japs put too much insecticide on the lettuce in order to poison the people of our country". People really hated all things Japanese during those times.

No one ever thought that a good percentage of those "Japs" were good citizens of the USA. The government and the media said that they were our enemies and were a clear and present danger to us and most people believed the story. Stoic Japanese Americans were rounded up and whole families were trucked off to internment camps. No one knew or cared about what happened to their homes or possessions. They were the enemy, end of story.

In reality the "Japs" were wonderful truck farmers and out performed the "round eyed" farmers hands down. Sure, some used the new pesticide DDT but so did everyone else. Rounding them up and placing them in camps hurt the vegetable farm sales a lot and made choices for the American housewife much more onerous.

One day my Dad brought home an avocado for Mom to prepare for the family. Now my Mom was a mid-westerner and had never before seen an avocado. Dad never said anything about the weird fruit but just set it on the kitchen sink. Mom was always up to the task at hand so she started to peel the avocado. The more she peeled the more she saw "green". Figuring that "green" meant that the "fruit" was not ripe she continued to peel. When she got to the large seed she figured that the "eating part" had to be inside the seed. Accordingly, she cracked the seed and, of course, found nothing. She gathered up the entire residue and threw it away. She never reported her introduction to an avocado until much later. I was an adult when she told me of her experience with the avocado. I think I laughed for days over that tale.

My mother became homesick for her Mom and sister and decided to take a trip home to Terre Haute, Indiana about this time. Money was always a problem at our house so it was decided that travel by bus was the best, most economical mode of travel. Airplanes were for rich folks and we were far from that. Mom packed a suitcase for herself and me and we sat off on our adventure.

The buses were primitive, at least most of them were. The seats were hard and uncomfortable and the trip was boring for a young boy. I imagine that it was boring for Mom also but she didn't complain like I did. Periodically the driver would stop at one of the "rest" stops where everyone could stretch and use the rest rooms. The rest stops were primitive also. There was very little to eat and Mom tried to stretch every dollar to the limit. There were no candy bars or comic books. Those items were frivolous.

The trip took four days and five nights. Think about it. Four days and five nights on a hard bench seat with little heat on the whole bus. We never laid our heads down once during that grueling time. We caught catnaps on the uncomfortable bus or in some of the bus terminals where we had to wait to transfer to some other bus. The bus terminals were generally run down and populated with less than desirable people. My mother took pains to keep me near her and watched carefully whenever I had to use the public restrooms. I'll never forget that ordeal. No motels, no TV, no upscale restaurants, no perks of any kind. Just plain, brutal travel.

When we crossed the Rocky Mountains it became cold. In some of the more primitive busses the flooring was all in one level. The heating systems were primitive and gave off very little heat except in the front of the bus. When the temperature dropped in those busses your feet became very cold. Imagine, if you can, having to sit immobile for hours while your feet became colder and colder. We used to try to sit on our feet but our legs quickly became numb. There were no blankets or anything else to cover our legs with. We had to stoically bear the cold. I complained, of course, but Mom seemed to be made of steel. She did whatever she could to make me comfortable but there was really nothing to be done. We were pleasantly surprised to find that some of the busses had a two-tiered floor. In those busses you walked to your seat on one level and stepped up to your seat on the other level. My feet were kept a lot warmer on those busses. Unfortunately the two-tiered busses were few and far between so Mom and I had to simply bear whatever pain was handed out to us.

We spent a week in Terre Haute and then repeated the bus trip in return. I'm sure that if my mother became homesick after that she kept the feelings to herself.

Sometime during this time period my family had a new arrival. I had a new sister. My mother enlisted an aunt to take care of me while she mysteriously disappeared in order to find my sister. It was all very confusing. My aunt tried very hard to make friends with me but she just didn't understand kids, having none of her own. She took me shopping thinking that would make me happy in spite of the disappearance of my parents. She promised me that I could have any toy I wanted. Of course I chose a toy gun that shot sparks when you wound it up and pulled the trigger. When I shot her with it she panicked over the sparks and pronounced it not fit for a child. I finally had to settle for a rubber knife, a poor substitute for a budding military hard case. I never forgave her for it. When I finally got home I found that I had a sister, whatever that was.

My sister was a real pain. She made lots of noise and received 100% of the attention in the family. The only good side about the whole episode was that I could finally pee outside without the fear of someone in the family spying on me and finding out that I had transgressed since my whole family's attention was concentrated on my new sister.

In later years I had occasion to talk to many mothers so I am sure that I was not the only boy who was a real pain in the posterior. That having been said I am honestly going to report several episodes that my mother related to me about my conduct. I can hardly give them credence but the only alternative is to call my mother a prevaricator so I will withhold comment and relay the story as it was told to me.

As the story goes one day my mother had occasion to use the facilities in the house. She allowed me to run free as she expected her visit to the toilet to be short. Inevitably, the doorbell rang while she was indisposed. I had been cautioned on innumerable times not to answer the door but the attention span and the memory of a five-year old is very short. I answered the door in spite of my mother yelling for me not to do so. A salesman stood in the door and asked, "Hi! Is your mother at home?"

In spite of the protestations of Mom I ran to the toilet, caught a glimpse of her and ran back to the salesman to report, "Yes, she's on the toilet." As the salesman strangled to contain his laughter I ran back to see what my Mom was yelling about. Again I caught a glimpse of her as she unsuccessfully tried to grab me, and immediately ran back to the door to report, "Just a minute. Just a minute. She's wiping now."

My Mom finally became mobile, succeeded in trapping me and placing me in another room and, red-faced, walked over to face the salesman who by now was having a hard time breathing while he unsuccessfully attempted to contain his laughter. Mom never reported just what he was selling or if he made a sale that day.

I guess, from all reports, that I was a rather sassy kid. At least I started out that way. Mom told of the time she was trying to correct me and had been unsuccessful. She had just corrected me verbally and instead of complying I had sassed her. She patiently repeated the correction to no avail. After the third attempt I ran over to a hallway, bent over and stuck out my tongue screaming, "Ya! Ya! Ya!" Mom says at the third "Ya" she sailed out of the room she was in and connected with a beautiful open-handed right cross. It landed squarely on my face and I took a double header that would have made the flying Wallendas in the circus proud. Mom says that I never tried to duplicate that faux pas. Apparently I had no trouble learning.

Kids have to try new things. It's all part of the learning process. One time I attempted to cannibalize my Mom, at least that is the way she tells it. I had found myself, for some reason, near her ankle. It apparently seemed like a good idea at the time because I took a good bite on her Achilles tendon. She reacted instantly and kicked me into the next room. Once again, the Wallendas would have signed me up if they had seen my act. I never repeated that act again either.

I can honestly never remember my Mom disciplining me by "counting to three" like modern day Moms do with their children. My Mom was an advocate of direct, sudden punishment for infractions, sort of like mother bears mete out to their kids. Now I can't vouch for all kids of my time but in my own case the punishment was extremely effective and the learning curve I experienced was steep. I had absolutely no trouble at all figuring out what was permissible and what was not.

I can recall the time I had found a penny and, like all children have done since time immemorial, I placed it in my mouth. Mom immediately made me spit it out and, once she had rinsed my mouth with water, she told me that I was not to repeat that particular trick, especially with coins. She said that coins were very, very dirty and even, as she said, "could have been in a nigger's pocket". That seemed to clinch it for Mom.

There was that word again. Nigger. I had not forgotten the little boy who had won the undeclared war between us with one blow when I had mentioned that word in his presence. I was not a particularly slow learner and I associated that word with all sorts of unpleasantries. Who knows? Perhaps I still unconsciously do today.

The school I attended was a no-nonsense institution. There was a time for everything and when everything was over it was time to go home. There was no lollygagging around on the playground after school. An elderly teacher was either appointed to police the playground or was a self appointed policeman but in any case it became fun for the kids to scurry under the fence and play on the swings before she noticed them. Of course I was one of the miscreants who would slither under the fence in order to dare the ogre who guarded the swings. No one knew just what dire punishment would be meted out if anyone were to be caught but there were lots of conjectures about what would happen. We would happily swing for a few minutes until the teacher would come screaming out of the school waving her hands in the air. Some of us would time her stumbling run and would run off ourselves just prior to being caught. It was exhilarating for young kids to bait the dragon in this manner.

One day she cheated. She enlisted the services of some older kids to help her catch the miscreants. We became aware of the change in tactics when the door to the school exploded with several "big" kids who could really run. With shouts of alarm the sinners abandoned the swings and ran for their lives. I was not genetically constituted to be a sprinter. The other kids were miles ahead of me in an instant. With my adrenalin topping out I ran for my life. I became the target as the other kids easily outdistanced me. The older kids were rapidly gaining on me. My lungs were on fire as I pumped my leaden legs. Finally one of the older kids jubilantly knew his prey was about to be caught. He thought to complete his kill by shouting, "Stop, kid, or I'll throw this rock!" I glanced behind in terror and saw that he had a large rock in one hand. Now I had never been trained in escape and evasion at that time in my life but somehow I intuitively knew that a moving target was harder to hit than a stationary one. Adrenalin gave me a burst of speed and with inches to spare I threw myself under the fence, tearing my clothes as I did so. Safe on the other side I paused to shout invectives at my torturers who threw their rocks in frustration. The rocks bounced harmlessly off of the fence.

No one attempted to use the swings after school following that harrowing experience for at least two weeks.

As kids will do, all of the kids I knew improvised a lot when it came to toys. Money was in short shrift in 1942 and kids didn't have the toys that modern day kids have. Marbles were precious. Only the "rich" kids had marbles that they were willing to risk losing in a game of "marbles". Most of the rest of us played "caps". This game depended on the little cardboard caps that topped the milk bottles that were used during this era. Kids would save the milk bottle caps and would play with them. The game was played by all of the players putting one bottle cap into a circle. Then the players would take turns throwing their "shooter" caps onto the caps in the circle. If you touched one of the caps in the circle with your "shooter" you could keep that cap. The game had all of the fascination of "marbles" but none of the expense.

Then there were the quaint customs of that time like "cuts" and "dibs". "Cuts" was invoked when a kid wished to bump into a line somewhere ahead of the end of the line. The kid acknowledging the "cut" would allow the interloper to move into the line ahead of him. Sometimes this would precipitate a fistfight because the kids behind the kid allowing the cut didn't recognize the custom. "Dibs" was an unsavory custom whereby a kid would approach another who was eating a candy bar or an ice cream cone. The pronouncement "Dibs" was supposed to be enough to allow the interloper to take a bite out of the "goodie" the possessor was eating. Happily this foray into socialism was short lived and didn't carry over into the later grades.

It was about this time in my life that I discovered sex. At least I discovered that little girls were constructed differently than little boys. There were several girls who lived near me. They were just slightly older than I was and one day I found myself with two sisters who challenged me. They told me that girls "pee-pees" were different than those possessed by boys and wanted to show me. Part of the equation was that I had to show them my "pee-pee". We accomplished that task with the end result that the girls announced that their "pee-pees" were prettier than mine was. An argument ensued since I discovered that I was competitive. We argued for several minutes with neither side being convinced that their opponent's argument was valid. Finally we tucked our prospective organs away and called it a draw. I have to smile whenever I think of that encounter. Later on in my life encounters like these were much more productive and satisfying.

My father continued with his job with the Bay City Transit Company in Santa Monica. He was assigned to the night shift and drove each evening until the line shut down for the night. He fell into the habit of carrying a pint of whiskey to work each evening. Maybe he was still grieving over his brother but at any rate no one ever knew the cause. He told me much later in life that he used to drink half of the bottle before starting to work each evening. That got him to the end of the line near the seashore on his first circuit. There he would drain the bottle discarding it in a trashcan. That seemed to calm him for the rest of his shift. This went on for some time.

Dad told me that he used to have to count the streetlights during some of the foggy nights when the fog was pea soup thick; so thick that it was impossible to read the street signs. It was important to know just where he was on his route as it ended at the waters edge. One night he lost count and drove his bus into the Pacific Ocean. It wasn't as serious as it might seem as he simply drove over the beach and into the water, not off of a pier into deep water. I think that episode might have caused him to rethink his drinking habits as he ceased to drink on the job after that.

There were many rumors about the war. I can remember my folks talking about the Japanese people who lived in California at that time. Mom used to carefully wash all of our vegetables very thoroughly as one of the rumors was that the "Japs" would put lots of insecticide on all of the vegetables in the hope that some Americans would become sick and even die. Nobody ever noticed that the "Japs" were American citizens too.

I learned about ration stamps and tokens. Critical items for sale had to be paid for with not only money but ration "points" also. The "points" were measured with stamps and tokens that had the point system printed on them. Each merchant that dealt in any kind of produce or items that were on the rationing list had to not only collect money for the items in question but also had to collect the required ration points for that item. Each month every family was allotted a certain amount of ration points for meat, gasoline, sugar, cooking oils and any other item labeled critical to the war effort. When you ran out of ration points for the month you could not purchase any more of that item regardless of how much money you had. My family never had the problem of having more money than ration points so the whole issue was academic as far as we were concerned. Some families would run out of ration points for things like sugar or oils. At times like those they would approach Mom and ask if she would give them her unused points, which she would readily do. Of course, according to the government, that was illegal but Mom, being a good, solid Scots lady, didn't give much of a crap about what the government thought. Mom was always a sentient, feeling person so she usually gave the supplicants any extra ration points that she had.

Some people sold any excess ration points they happened to have left over. It was illegal to do so but it happened more often than not. Things were hard during the war and every family had to sacrifice for the war effort so few families were reported for violating the edict against selling rationing certificates.

My father finally found a job at the Consolidated Aircraft Company building airplanes. It was a much better job than being a bus driver and it paid better. Shortly after he found the job all war effort jobs were "frozen". By frozen it was meant that you were not supposed to be able to leave your job for anything until the war was over. It made sense to most of the people who worked at Consolidated but didn't make much sense to the folks who had been slaves prior to the end of the Civil war. My folks apparently thought that the "work freeze" wasn't all that much different from the policies of the outfit we were supposed to be fighting, like those of Herr Hitler and his slave labor battalions. When it comes right down to it, serfs are serfs. It really doesn't make much difference what you call the working multitudes. That worked OK for most people but my mother missed the Midwest and her folks and really wished to return. In all truth my father probably felt much the same way. A lot of midnight oil was expended along with a lot of discussion about the future between my parents. Finally it was decided that the family had to return to Terre Haute. Freedom triumphed.

Dad gave his notice to sever his association with Consolidated. He was threatened with legal processes but he did not waiver from his intended course and finally Consolidated allowed him to leave. The family car was packed and we were on our way. We made slow time across the country. We stopped several times at points of interest, the Sequoia National Forest to see the giant trees, the Petrified Forest to see the old, dead trees, the desert, the mountains. I learned about the wonderful country I lived in and learned to hate the Japs and the Germans who wanted to destroy it all. That trip with my parents did much to enlarge my education. I've never forgotten it. We had several flat tires on the way. Rubber was a critical item also and tires were expensive and in short supply. My father stoically fixed each flat with a small kit he had packed in the trunk. After he had repaired the tear in the tire he then had to pump up the tire with a hand pump.

Tires at that time consisted of two pieces. There was the tire proper, the outside, the part that you could see, the part that hit the road. Then there was an inner part or an inner tube that was made of rubber and that actually held the air inside the tire. Usually, when a tire was punctured, it was the inner tube that was damaged. The inner tube was much more pliable and repairable than the rough outside "tire" was. Dad could repair the inner tube with a kit that involved a rubber-sulfur patch that had to be lighted with a match after it had been carefully placed over the puncture. The resulting flame would anneal the patch to the tube, sealing it and then the tube could be pumped back up after it had been replaced inside the tire.

It took a long time but time seemed to be the easiest thing to come by at that time in history. Triple A had not been thought of and even if it had my family would not have had enough money to join that club. Calling a tow truck was for rich folk so it was not feasible. Have you ever tried to pump up a car tire with a hand pump? It's not like pumping up a bicycle tire. It seems to take days but my folks stoically accomplished it. Whenever I think of that I'm reminded of the old Zen riddle that goes, "How do you eat an elephant?" The answer is, "One bite at a time." When you have to do something and there are no alternatives you will be surprised at what you can actually accomplish. Think about ants and what they accomplish. The trip seemed to take forever for a young boy. Nights were a problem. My parents never had much money and what motels there were always cost a lot; at least as far as we were concerned. We stayed in a few rat-hole motels and more often than not we slept in the car when everyone got tired. Sometimes the motel we stopped at would accept kids but not animals. Some would accept animals but not kids. I can remember Dad coming back to the car very angry and telling us, "They said that they would take the dog but not the kids so I told them I was going to shoot the kids and keep the dog." We ended up sleeping in the car. Eventually we reached Indiana and Grandma Issler put us up until we could find suitable lodgings.

On our way to Terre Haute a sad episode happened, at least it was sad as far as I was concerned. We had stopped at a large gas station complex in Nevada that boasted not only gasoline but also a restaurant and a small store. My folks were planning on having dinner at the restaurant. As we got out of the car my Dad remarked that he could hear an elk bugling in the hills behind the complex. We forgot about it until the owner of the complex entered the restaurant dragging a large elk that he had shot. The elk had its tongue hanging out and was dripping blood from a large hole in its shoulder and from its mouth. The man who had shot it was very proud and said, "Folks, I heard him whistling earlier and I decided to bag him. If you'll just give me a few minutes I'll have some beautiful elk steaks and roasts for sale." I was very young but it struck me as unfair that the man had shot the elk just to be able to sell a few steaks to strangers. A beautiful animal had been dispatched just to put a few dollars in his pocket. I was disgusted and I didn't even know what disgust was back then. Little did I know that I was an incipient tree hugger at a time that tree hugger was not really in our vocabulary.

We arrived in Terre Haute and my folks found a rental home across the street from my maternal grandparents, which was fortuitous, as the Landers needed as much help as they could get. Initially I attended an upscale school named Davis Park Elementary. After around six months or so the school districts changed and I was forced to switch to a new school called Thompson Elementary. Apparently Davis Park was higher on the food chain than Thompson because I was subjected to quite a lot of mud slinging and innuendoes because of my prior attendance at the more elite school. It was very confusing as I never could figure out just what I had done wrong whenever some teacher would look down her nose at me and remark, "Well! Is that the way they do things at Davis Park?" I became the whipping boy for everything that was seen as wrong with Davis Park. I accepted the hair shirt as just something that I had to put up with. My parents had raised me to accept things and to not question the rocks that were put in my pathway through life.

Once back in Terre Haute I had ample opportunity to socialize with both sets of grandparents. One evening we spent the night with my paternal grandparents and several of my father's siblings. We had to double up on the available beds and I was allotted a makeshift bed on the floor along with Dad's younger brother, Murray.

I was awakened sometime during the night by a hand groping my genitals. I didn't know what to make of the whole thing. It was 1942 and the subject of sex was not broached to children until they were in their teens, if then. I had no ideas at all concerning sex let alone sex of the homosexual variety. Having no idea what this was all about and, as it felt soothing, I elected to pretend to stay asleep. Murray fondled my genitals for a while and finally rolled over and went to sleep. I was six years old at the time.

Later on in life I read that in some of the more primitive societies mothers would fondle the genitals of their children in order to calm them down and to keep them from crying. That was hardly the case here. During this period it was unheard of for parents to discuss episodes like this with their children and to prompt them as to what action to take if any one attempted to molest them.

I was embarrassed by the whole episode and, since I didn't seem to be injured at all I decided not to relate anything concerning it to either of my parents. I never did.

Much later in life Murray's lifestyle became an open book. He cohabited with another male for a long time and finally died of AIDS. He was always odd and his lifestyle fitted with his fey behavior. He became the family embarrassment.

I used to tease my Dad about him.

"How's queer Uncle Murray doing these days?"

"That's not very nice." This from Dad.

"I know it's not nice. So why's he do it?"

"That's not what I mean and you know it." And so on.

I always thought it strange that the only homosexual insult I ever suffered came from a family member.

Thompson Elementary was a lot more comfortable than Davis Park. I liked the school. It was not pretentious at all and suited me a lot better than the more ostentatious school. Every morning all of the students congregated in the gymnasium to sing "Carry Me Back to Ole Virginny", a Stephen Foster song about the south. Even with my limited knowledge of geography I wondered why a school in Indiana had adopted that song as its apparent hallmark. I never knew the answer to that question.

World War II was in its ascendancy at this time and the school hosted many paper drives and "tin can collections" for use in the war. The "tin cans" had to have both ends cut out and laid inside the tube, which was then stomped into a flat mass of metal. The cans and the papers were then weighed and the student who had delivered them was issued several stamps depending on the weight of the offerings. The stamps could then be stuck on a large picture of either Hitler or Tojo, depending on the student's choice. Acceptable targets for the stamps were the despot's eyes, nose or mouth, the object being to cover the whole picture.

We were taught that the enemy, whether Jap or German, were not really humans like we were. They were "something else" and, as such, were fair game for anything we wanted to do with them. Much later on in life I learned that the attitudes we were taught were taught to each military person who went into harms way. If you thought that the enemy wasn't human it was much easier to kill them. That worked for the military and still does. Easily enough the same thought patterns work for offshoot outfits like the Ku Klux Klan and the various militant white power groups that exist.

School at Thompson was easy and pleasurable. I found the subjects interesting and soon settled into a routine. One of the boys in my class had some insurmountable problems with reading. He couldn't seem to be able to recognize any of the words even after they were repeated several times. He was a friend of mine and I stuck by him even though most of the other kids abandoned him just like animals would abandon one of their flock or herd that was damaged in some way. I really think that I was the only friend he had and I used to agonize over his futile attempts to pronounce the words that he was supposed to read to the class. The way reading was taught at that time was for the student to read to the class from the front of the class. That put you at the tip of the spear and any mistake you might make was readily apparent to the rest of the class. Mistakes were met with ready ridicule notwithstanding the efforts of the teacher to calm the hoots and catcalls. My friend had to withstand lots of ridicule every day. The teacher was oblivious to the harassment.

"All right, Herbert, Please read to the class from the third paragraph."

Herbert stood silently in front of the class holding his book in front of his face and adopting a face screwed up with effort.

"Herbert, please read now."

No response.

"Herbert, the first word is Christopher." The teacher attempted to be helpful.

"Christopher" Herb was trying.

"Yes, Herbert, that's right. Now what is the second word?"

No response.

"Answered" the exasperated teacher offered.

"Answered", Herb reluctantly said. The pauses between words grew longer. The teacher had no answers for the problem. No one did at that time. It was the state of the art in the teaching profession at the time.

"Buh", Herbert pronounced triumphantly. The sentence read, "Christopher answered, 'the dog did it!'"

"Yes, Herbert, yes! The next word is indeed 'the'." Herb beamed at the praise. The students hooted and nudged each other winking and smiling.

At recess several of the kids surrounded Herb poking fun at him and calling him a "dummy". I intervened and offered to beat up on anyone who wanted to stick around. Everyone judiciously departed the area. Herb smiled at his savior and said, "I did good today didn't I Eddie? I read 'buh'". I agreed with him since I didn't have the answers any more than the teacher did. I only knew that he was my friend and I would stick up for him. I never knew what happened to my friend. I can only hope that he coped somehow and made his way in the world in the best way that he possibly could. In the final analysis this is all any of us can do. Teachers, government, family can only give support. It's the same thing that a school of fish does. The school is there to give support to the group. Any predator will get confused due to the plethora of targets and perhaps miss its target. The individual is not considered in this module. The consideration is only for the group. The same thing is true for humans and their groupings. The government mandated schools can only "teach" (or more importantly "indocrinate") the populace. Individuals may be very intellegent but, for some reason, have difficulty in certain areas like reading or math. The system doesn't care. The police exist only to keep the general peace. They do not and are not responsible for the safety of individuals in the society. In the final analysis we are all on our own. The responsibility for our well-being is solely on our own heads. Police groups are "historians" according to a good friend of mine. They come on scene after the deed has been done and take pictures and measurements but in no way do they prevent any malfeasance.

This is our society and, in the long run, perhaps it serves to strengthen the group in much the same way that flocks of animals, birds and schools of fish do. The weak and damaged among us never really succeed just as the weak and damaged among the animal kingdom die early or are preyed upon by preditors. Do we differ that much from the animals?

One day the teacher gave me a note to take home to my parents. I had absolutely no knowledge as to what the note was all about and the courtesy my parents had taught me prevented me from questioning the teacher. I suspected that I was in trouble over something as that was usually the reason why kids got to take a note home to Mom.

When she read the note my Mom took a long hard look at me reinforcing the idea I had of being in some sort of trouble. I couldn't imagine just what I had done but it wasn't at all unusual for me to have stepped over some line or other violating some edict. I had always carried a pocketknife and considered that to be the norm for boys of my age in that time of my life. Occasionally some little girl would discover that I had a knife when I used it to sharpen a pencil or clean my fingernails. Usually the little girl would tell the teacher that "Eddie has a knife" and the teacher would make me stay after school along with promising to "never, never bring a knife to school ever again". I always promised but the next day would see me with one or two of my favorite knives in my pockets once again. I was not unusual. Every boy carried a knife at this time in our history. Knives were not considered to be weapons. They were tools and were used as tools several times a day.

The next day Mom accompanied me to school. I figured, "Boy, it must be really serious." I just hoped that it wouldn't mean some sort of demeaning embarrassment that would give the other kids ammunition for further harassment. The fact that Mom didn't say anything to me about the note was another giveaway to the seriousness of the problem. Usually small problems gave rise to a lot of yelling and the liberal application of my father's leather belt. Larger problems made serious lectures necessary accompanied, of course, by lots of yelling and the liberal use of my father's belt. This sounded like the serious kind simply because it was unusual in that there was no yelling or carrying on of any type.

My Mom talked to the teacher for a long time. Finally I was called to account. Both adults told me that they thought that I was working in a grade that was too easy for me and that I could profit by being put in the next higher grade immediately. They asked me if I minded going to the higher grade. I was so elated by not being punished I readily agreed to whatever they suggested. The teacher took me to another room filled with strangers and introduced me to another teacher and that was that.

I hadn't learned a thing since kindergarten. Mom was ever ready to place me into some school with a bunch of strangers via some scam or other. Once again I was a prisoner.

The new class wasn't much of a problem as far as reading went but arithmetic was an entirely different thing. I had been used to adding a series of numbers no larger than hundreds. Now I was required to not only add columns of numbers in the thousands and hundreds of thousands but to do so in a timely manner. Not only that, but the students were required to get up in front of the class and go over their work verbally.

"One and three are four plus six is ten plus eight is eighteen plus nine is twenty-seven. Put down the seven and carry the two. Six and seven is . . . ." And so it went. I wasn't used to doing sums as fast as that so often I found myself in front of the class having to do the problem in my head since I had not completed the written assignment yet. I wasn't very fast on my feet so I appeared as the class dummy; at least it seemed like that to me. I was very uncomfortable and I had no real friends, as I was much younger than any of the other kids. I became a loner, once again. Being a loner was becoming a normal thing for me. I was really unused to having any friends at all let alone a good buddy that I could count on.

One day I was treated to a fine example of man's inhumanity to man. I was walking home from school when I turned a corner and encountered a fistfight by two bigger boys. One of the boys was obviously better trained than the other. Even a novice like me could tell that the underdog was outmatched. He was taking three blows for every one he gave and the hits he took were expertly applied and telling. As I stood there with an open mouth gawking at the melee an adult appeared on the scene. I expected him to break up the fight but he stood on the sidelines and cheered the best fighter.

"Atta boy, Jack. Hit him hard. Now uppercut! Uppercut! Knock him out. Work his stomach. Bury your fist in him. Hit him harder, Kill him, Jack, Kill him."

I was appalled. Other than protecting myself I had always been taught that fighting was prohibited. My disciplinarian father would not countenance cowardliness neither would he countenance aggression. I had never before seen an adult egg on a fight. It scared and sickened me. I felt immediately sorry for the underdog but couldn't do anything about it. I watched him be beaten into the ground and watched the adult congratulate the winner and walk off with his arm around that kid's shoulder while the loser had to pick himself off the ground and go home alone. I never forgot that incident and resolved to correct any others I happened upon if I had the means to do so. The whole incident also made me think that I could not count on any outside help if I was ever the subject of any attack on my person. It made me think a little about just how I would handle something like that in order to preserve myself. I think that I was probably around seven at the time.

Mom always had a temper. It was often manifested when she attempted to extricate a pot or frying pan from the drawer under the cooking stove. Apparently there were too many pots and pans in the drawer and they would become entangled. Mom would try to pull one out. When that wasn't working she would become red in the face. The veins in her neck would stand out and she would grit her teeth. She would redouble her efforts and the result was a massive tug of war between her and the pots. Her efforts were always very noisy and whenever she was successful in extricating a pot she would throw it across the room in anger. The din was horrible. The poor dog, who bedded down under the table, would try vainly to run away from the melee but the kitchen floor, made up of linoleum, would not allow that. The dog would run as fast as he could but wouldn't go anywhere, as the slick floor didn't allow him any purchase. I can remember feeling very sorry for Ted as he tried in vain to escape the noisy battleground with the flying pots and pans. Thinking back on the episodes concerning my Mom's temper I am convinced that I have the same genes that made her temper erupt. The big difference is that I am empathetic toward my dogs and always do my best to make sure that the poor guys don't have to operate in an aura of terror with flying pots and pans.

One day Mom's temper got the best of her. Apparently I was underfoot while she was attempting to make supper for the family. I had been told several times to go somewhere else but, of course, I paid no attention to the warnings. All of a sudden she reached her limit as far as obnoxious kids go. She used the only weapon she had available and hit me on the head with a heavy spatula. Unfortunately the spatula edge cut my head and, as head wounds, however slight, are apt to do it bled profusely. Initially I was very angry as the damned spatula hurt but the cries of my horrified mother alarmed me. She saw the amount of blood that had spurted on the walls and thought that she had killed me. Her screams scared me and when I saw the blood I was frightened all the more. We both were quite a spectacle, standing there amid all the blood, yelling and screaming at each other. Mom panicked and took me to a hospital where the cut was sutured and the bleeding stopped. Everyone calmed down and whatever I had done to precipitate the incident was forgotten. Just another day in the Lander's family routine and I actually got to see the inside of a hospital.

Oh! And the police were not called and Mom was not arrested for child abuse and incarcerated. People at that time had brains and actually used them.

My parents had made friends with a family in Clinton, Indiana who owned a farm. We used to visit them on a Saturday about once a month. The family had four boys and the usual amount of farm animals along with several dogs and cats. I loved the farm and the company and tagged along with the boys as they tramped through the woods and fields. It was a super way to spend a Saturday.

One day while we were jumping across a fast moving stream I picked what looked like a dry sand bar to hop on. When I jumped on it I immediately sank up to my chest in quicksand. I panicked and yelled for help. The other boys saw that I was not sinking any further so they stood around laughing and poking fun at me. Apparently I had hit a solid bottom so I was in no real danger. I finally pulled myself out and went to the farm house to dry out.

One Saturday one of the younger boys wanted to show me something. He took me to one of the tall hedges that surrounded the house and parted the leaves to show me a tiny nest with four little sparrows in it. When the baby birds heaard the noise of the hedge leaves being disturbed they all opened their beaks awaiting their parents with food. It was a wonderful glimpse of nature. My friend cautioned me not to tell anyone about the nest. He said that his Mom would insist that the babies be "given to the cat" as she hated the sparrows that hung around the farm. I promised but one of the bigger boys had spied on us and immediately told his Mom. The tough old farm lady called all of the boys together and demanded that the baby birds be given to the cat in spite of entreaties from the young boys. Amid loud protests and crying the biggest boy picked up the cat and we all went to the hedge that contained the nest. The boy picked the nest up and, one by one, he tossed the protesting birds on the ground where the cat made quick work of them. When the cat tired of the game it tortured the last of the little birds before eating them. I watched the slaughter in horror. I couldn't believe that any one would blandly take an innocent life, human or animal; to kill one of God's creatures coldly and calmly for no real purpose. That whole scene made a big impression on me as a very young boy that has lasted a lifetime.

About this time period my paternal grandparents were undergoing difficulties. My grandfather, Noah Levi, was not only a disciplinarian but also a Tatar to boot. He beat his children, he beat his wife and he would have beat his dog if any dog could be found that would put up with such nonsense. His family made fun of him behind his back. He had lost all respect, love and loyalty but was too stupid to realize that fact. His meek but stalwart wife finally filed for divorce, something that was not entered into lightly in the 1940s.

I can distinctly remember my father asking my grandfather to leave his house when Grandpa Landers sought to enlist Dad's help in the divorce. I thought it was a sad day for the family; sad but necessary, as Grandma Landers moved to California with the bulk of her family to remain there until her death many years later.

Grandpa Noah burned his bullheaded way through several other wives, each of them taking a piece of his estate as they divorced him. He finally died and was buried in Lakeland, Florida; requiescat in pace. Noah used to say that he had suffered more pain than Jesus had since Jesus only existed on earth for 36 years and Noah had lived for twice that. Perhaps he was right. I always felt sorry for him, not for what he said but for what he didn't know. He was successful in a way but was ignorant in so many other ways. He was my grandfather and I own some of his genes. It's a scary thought.

My father was never what you would call a raving success at anything. He did a lot of soul-searching and finally decided to become a minister or a preacher. Whatever you call it he wished to extend the gospel of Christ to the millions and so he decided to attend the Bible Baptist Seminary at Fort Worth, Texas. It was an old established seminary for Southern Baptists and it catered to relatively undereducated men like Dad.

I really never knew what my father did for a living in Terre Haute but whatever it was he left it to move his family to Fort Worth, Texas. As part of his family I, of course, trailed along.

Chapter Two

We arrived at Fort Worth in the summer. It was hot in "Cow Town" and accommodations were sparse, especially for a seminarian with no job or funds. Dad found a friend who had a house trailer, now called a mobile home, who was willing to put his family up for a month or two until better accommodations could be found. The friend had a family of his own, a wife and two children, ages much the same as ours. The trailer was a 1940s version, tiny, with a "kitchen" but no bath. It was about 24 feet long at the longest. Eight people cohabited in that tiny trailer for a couple of months in the name of God. We would all go to the showers furnished by the trailer park in order to bathe. All of the kids thought it was a lark, little did we know. I personally loved the other family. They were kind and caring and the time I spent in that tiny trailer is fond in my memories. I don't think that you've really lived until you share a 24-foot house trailer with seven other people for a month or two.

One Saturday both families treated themselves by going to the zoo. It was a wonderful time for a young boy, full of unfamiliar sights and amazing animals. Mr. Howzel, the father of the family we were staying with, thought that it was great fun to tease and torment the animals. He had a large audience since he was very vocal and animated and several groups of people paused to watch his antics. He began with the monkeys that were housed in a large cage. He mugged for them until he got the attention of the largest monkey, the apparent leader of the tribe. Mr. Howzel held the bars of the cage with both hands and jumped up and down hooting as he did. It was a parody of the actions of the monkeys and seemed to be a challenge to the leader who reacted in exactly the same manner as his challenger. It was very funny watching the human and the primate scream at each other while they jumped up and down. Soon the whole tribe joined in the fray and the zoo erupted in chaos.

When Mr. Howzel tired of playing with the monkeys we all went to the lion exhibit. The monkeys celebrated their victory over him by screaming and racing around satisfied, apparently, by having chased their tormentor off. Howzel tried the same tactic with the lion that ignored him with regal disdain. The man tried to assuage his injured pride at being ignored by the animal by throwing garbage at the lion.

As I watched, the lion never bothered to acknowledge the man. He slowly turned his back on his tormentor and urinated a thick stream of odorous, yellow urine on the cement floor of his cage. As he did he used his back feet to throw the urine toward the humans who had dared to try to demean him for their pleasure. The crowd that had gathered to watch Howzel tease the lion ran away, the men laughing and the women screaming. The lion regally walked away and laid down watching the general melee. Howzel retired "hors combat" reeking of cat urine.

I watched in wonder at the tactics the animal used to defeat the human. Since then I have listened to the biologists and animal behaviorists who decry assigning human emotions and thought to animals, dismissing such ideas as anthropomorphism. I listen but do not believe. Animals have feelings and emotions. Any observant dog owner can attest to that. They also have intellect. We, as humans, fancy that we are the only organisms on our planet that are capable of cogent thought. That idea discounts animals as a whole especially dolphins, whales, dogs and cats among others. Just because an animal cannot complete one of our tests that purport to measure an "intelligence quotient" does not rule out an intelligence that we have not, as yet, been able to measure. We can all learn from the so called lesser life forms on our planet.

My family finally found a cheap rental place on the edge of town. It was primarily two little rooms with a bathroom. In later years it would be called a slum but it was immeasurably better than a cardboard box or the backseat of a car. My parents slept in the bedroom and my sister and I slept in the "living room". The living room substituted for a dining room and a kitchen. The kitchen consisted of a hot plate and a sink with running water. The toilet was an old fashioned one that had the water closet hung high, near the ceiling, and was operated by a pull chain. It was noisy and stank, as the plumbing was not modern enough to own a trap that would prevent sewer gas from entering the living spaces. My memories of that place are primarily ones of the foul smells emanating from that toilet.

The school I attended was nice. The only memories I have of that period are of a school chum whose family was of the Jehovah's Witness belief. They believed that prayer could solve all ills and refused to go to any doctors. My friend was a gentle soul and I really felt close to him. One day he revealed to me that his mother was sick and was believed to be dying. He was obviously distressed. I asked him what his family was doing for her and he said they were praying for her. I didn't understand that and asked my father about the situation. He explained to me that the faith my friend adhered to mandated prayer and nothing else for medical treatment. I didn't understand that and thought it to be a rather dumb approach to things but, once again, I was in the minority and couldn't do anything about the problem. I suffered with my friend and felt sorrow when his Mom died. As Dad explained it, it was God's will so anything that could have been done would have been to no avail anyway. Later on in life, when I became more worldly and impertinent, I would have termed that thought fatalistic and, well, dumb. Most religions mandate that God gives us the wonderful idea of a choice. In other words God allows us a choice in everything we do and believe in. In accordance with that idea if you choose to ignore modern medicine (or primitive medicine, for that matter) then the concept of God allowing you to choose still works but in the extreme case the patient dies. I don't agree with that idea but, once again, I'm probably in a minority position.

When the term lease ran out on the smelly apartment we moved to the living quarters of a rather noble woman who had a large apartment near town. She was a patrician lady and did not suffer children. I was cautioned not to talk to her or bother her in the least. I was intimidated.

The school I attended had Spanish language as a mandatory subject. My class was composed of at least 50% Mexican students. I always thought it patently unfair that the Mexicans could all get "A's" in Spanish while the rest of us got whatever we could get in the discipline. I also thought that the Mexicans were rough. They tended to be rude in class and were quick with their fists, something that I had always been taught to avoid. That attitude was beginning to be integral with me as time marched on. I avoided controversy and belligerence but it was an increasingly hard thing to accomplish.

One day a student I had always thought was a friend approached me. He told me that all of his friends thought that he was a sissy because he had befriended me. I had always been an outcast because I was a "Yankee". Now my "friend" told me that to stay in favor with his friends he had to "beat up on me a little". He said that he didn't want to do it but he really had to do so because if he didn't he would be an outcast. He asked if he could "just hit you a little on the shoulder to show that I can do it". Chump that I was, I agreed because he was "my friend".

My "friend" hit my shoulder hard enough to numb it. He walked away sneering and was welcomed by all of his peers who also sneered at me for not responding to the onslaught. I was alone and I learned from the incident. Don't believe anyone. Never allow anyone to touch, hit, harm or injure you. Don't believe anyone. Don't listen to words. Believe actions. Don't believe anyone. Above all, don't believe anyone but trust your instincts. I resolved to stand up for myself in the future and not to "be a chump" any longer. To hell with my Dad's edict not to be aggressive. It appeared that the only way to gain respect was to be aggressive. It was a lesson I never forgot. I really think that the incident was a turning point in my life.

I suddenly realized that other humans didn't really care for you or about you at all. Whether you lived or died made no difference to them at all. When I had occasion to really think about it I realized that aggression wasn't the only factor in the equation of respect and concern. The other factor was sudden, harsh and draconian measuring out of physical force and the more harsh the better. I was changed.

Later in life I became acquainted with a gentleman named Marcus Tulius Cicero. He lived from 106 to 53 B.C. He said, "There exists a law, not written down anywhere, but inborn in our hearts; a law which comes to us not by training or customs or reading; a law which has not come to us from theory but from practice, not by instruction but by natural intuition. I refer to that law which lays it down that if our lives are endangered by plots or violence or armed robbers or enemies, any and every method of protecting ourselves is morally right."

I've lived my life by that creed even before I knew of this gentleman.

The only friend I found in Fort Worth, Texas was the city library. I found it by accident one day and was enthralled by the gigantic assortment of information you could find in that beautiful building. I immediately quit looking for "friends" and began checking out voluminous amounts of books on every subject imaginable. At first the librarians were suspicious of me but as the books were well cared for and always returned on time or earlier they finally accepted me for a kindred spirit who simply loved books and the information they could impart.

As my father was attending the seminary for ministers we, of course, spent a good deal of our time at the Bible Baptist Church and Seminary. We attended Wednesday evening prayer meetings and a variety of meetings that had to do with missionary work spreading the good word. Kids were tolerated but there was nothing much for them to do other than to "shut up and stay out of the way". We mostly learned how to do that with alacrity. Baptists were not known for sparing the rod and spoiling the child. Highlights of each evening were when you could partake of the apple cider and doughnuts furnished for all of the seminarians.

The head of the church and seminary was a stalwart figurehead who was the epitome of Southern gentry. Tall and erect he was always an imposing figure. J. Frank Norris was a no-nonsense preacher who made no apology concerning his beliefs. I have seen him call for the black janitors who took care of the church, asking them to come to the pulpit with him. He would then put his arms around the gentlemen and tell his parishioners, "These are my niggers. I love my niggers. They're the best in the whole world." The black gentlemen would smile and accept the accolades.

My mother bought into the whole idea. She loved to call black people "niggers". She always said, "We always call them niggers down south. They don't mind down there." I knew better. I would always remember the response of the little kindergartener who knocked me into the dirt when I mistakenly hailed him with, "Hi, nigger."

J. Frank preached not only the word of God but also told his parishioners about his ideas concerning the "Japs". He was like one of the old Revolutionary ministers who preached against King George. He was right, of course, and his people loved him. Modern day ministers could profit from the tactics of J. Frank Norris. Don't you think that modern congregations would welcome some "from the heart" lectures concerning the forces that are antagonistic to our way of life? J. Frank Norris had some very hard ideas about the war and the government in general and told his congregation all about his ideas every Sunday. He was a refreshing, honest preacher. We loved him.

My first introduction to the Boy Scouts was in that church. My Father took me to a Scout meeting and I got to watch the Scouts "box the compass" and practice some first aid. I was impressed. Dad told me that when I got a little older I could join a scout group. I could hardly wait.

Dad finally found a rental house in the country to the north of Fort Worth. It had plenty of room both for a family and for a couple of kids who needed room to play. Most of the neighbors kept chickens, usually Bantams that were friendly and colorful. I used to play with Bantam chickens and horned toads. Between those playmates, books and the Tom Mix radio programs I was kept busy.

Along with the move to a different home I was shifted to another school. Different schools were beginning to be a way of life for me. In the present instance I not only became a stranger to the school, a risky business at best, but I was also the worst kind of outsider, a northerner.

Normally, whenever a new student checked into a new school he was faced with the monumental task of proving himself. Normally, again, this meant that he had to take on all comers who wished to protect the good name of the school by beating up on the "new kid". I never really knew why "the new kid" was a threat to the school but others did and I was in no position to argue with them. The only thing I could do was to fight as well as I could and let the chips fall where they may. I found out early on that the refusal to fight meant a life of torment while the willingness to fight coupled with a keen aggressiveness engendered a certain respect among the rest of the students. Indeed, if I could get the idea across that I was not only willing but also eager to kill my opponent I was generally left alone for the remainder of the school year. That attitude was one that has been continually relearned over and over again by a lot of countries the whole time I have been alive. Countries that have been willing to roll over and succumb to the chauvinism of other countries have always been overrun. Look at he history of the Second Word War, Germany, France, Belgium, Switzerland, and Czechoslovakia and see which countries survived and which didn't. I resolved not to be as ignorant or dumb as some of those countries.

Prior to discovering this startling concept I had been soundly beaten several times on the playground. I had resolved never to allow this to happen again.

When I checked into my new school I was greeted with the normal catcalls.

"Yankee".

"Asshole."

"Fuck you, Yankee."

The teacher ignored the catcalls. She imperiously assigned me a seat and told me to sit down and pay attention. My contemporaries sneered and promised to "get me" at recess. It was a very nice atmosphere for learning.

True to form, at the first recess I was faced with a circle of tormenters bent on making my life miserable. I had been beaten up so many times prior to this that I was generally inured to the ignominy of it all. I figured that I had nothing to lose and I resolved to make my tormentor pay dearly for my embarrassment. I assumed the position of a fighter and waited.

The biggest and best of the Indians circling my wagon faced me. He drew cheers when he made threats and maligned my family tree. I remained silent and on guard. He finally advanced and threw his finest punch, calculated to awe and flatten me. Instead of quailing I blocked his arm, stepped into his circle and hit him squarely on his nose drawing first blood. I had learned from prior fights.

To my amazement the blow drew cheers from the rooting section. They didn't care who won. All they wanted to see was blood. My opponent shook his head, snorted blood and snot and attacked with renewed vigor. It became readily apparent that he was an inept fighter and that he relied on his bulk and reputation to win his battles. It wouldn't work today. I stayed away from his charges and hit him each time he came near. He was fast becoming a mess of blood and roars as he threatened ineffectual things that he intended to do to me. The crowd was silent as they watched their hero.

I had retreated into the role of a quiet observer of the fight. I never made any noise but whenever my opponent came near I hit him as hard as I could and always on his face. He never landed a blow on me. He began blubbering and I let him go as long as he stayed away from me. Every now and then he would remember how tough he was and would charge me only to be hammered again. I began to feel sorry for him. The cheering section was silent and had begun to disperse.

It finally ended by my unworthy opponent saying that he would allow me to go. I waited until he had departed the area and only then did I drop my guard. No one else wanted to take me on after the show they had just witnessed. That was fine with me. I never wanted to fight in the first place.

I was never harassed again. Apparently I was known as a "stone killer" since I hadn't made any noise during the fight but just attended to business. It was a good lesson. It wasn't what your opponent really knew about you. It was what he thought about you that counted. If he thought that you were the toughest hombre west of the Mississippi far be it from you to dissuade him of that opinion. Quietly and suddenly administering harsh and painful punishment was the key to peace and the quicker the punishment was administered the better.

I was very proud of having soundly whipped a braggart Texan. I knew that I had made no friends by doing so but it didn't matter much. I never had many friends anyway.

The school was much the same as any other school in that kids were not allowed to make any noise. At lunchtime each student was required to eat his or her lunch on small bleachers in the school's gymnasium. The lunchtime was supposed to be a silent time. Talking was not allowed. Upper classmen stalked the ranks of silent eaters fixing them with silent stares. The upper classmen ate their sandwiches silently while stalking. Every once in a while they would find some sinner who was whispering to a neighbor. When this happened the "monitors" would point to the sinner in question and shout, "Back Row". The sinner so tagged would have to arise, gather his/her lunch and retire to the back row of the bleachers. The kids were excused by rows to be allowed to go to the playground and spend the rest of the lunch period there. Every one in the row to be excused had to be completely finished with their lunch before the row was "excused". The back row was the last row to be excused. This was the punishment for opening your mouth for anything other than to stuff part of your sandwich into it. In the year 2005 this would be termed torture if it were applied to prisoners in Guantanamo Bay, Cuba. In 1947 kids were apparently exempt from the first amendment of the Constitution of the United States and could not voice an opinion or a dissent. Having given some thought to the quant custom centered around the consumption of lunch in that school the only conclusion I could come to was that the procedure was being taught so that the students would know how to conduct themselves in the event that they had to spend some time in a prison. Later on, say in 2007, those students would probably excel as members of the TSA.

Some of the kids I walked to school with lived on a ranch. They were worldly kids and knew all about sex. I knew absolutely nothing about sex but pretended that I did as the alternative was to be considered to be a real dummy. One day one of my friends asked me if I wanted to watch their bull breed cows. Of course I did. I had no idea what the bull did when he bred cows but considered this to be a learning experience. I showed up at the appointed place at the appointed time and awaited events.

The bull's name was, of course, Ferdinand. Ferdinand was in a small pen and was unconcerned about whatever was going to happen. A cow in estrus was introduced to Ferdinand who ignored her. I had no idea what estrus or heat or anything else was all about but watched wide-eyed as the cow made a complete idiot of herself by mounting Ferdinand, licking his very large scrotum and making a generally loud ruckus about the whole episode. The cowhands tried to encourage Ferdinand by throwing rocks at him and shouting, "C'mon Ferdinand." The old bull was singularly unimpressed.

Finally the bull got the idea, slowly sauntered over to the cow and leisurely mounted her. He entered her as I watched with awe and large eyes. He gave three thrusts and gave up to the renewed shouts of the cowhands accompanied by more missiles aimed at him. The cow went ballistic and tried vainly to explain to Ferdinand just what his function was in all of this. He merely blinked and chewed, telegraphing to everyone that he was too engrossed in meditation to be bothered by mundane things like this stupid cow.

The whole episode was repeated several times to the accompaniment of shouts, laughter and ribald jokes. I resolved not to tell my father about the incident fearing that he would rain abuse on my head for subjecting myself to something as worldly as Ferdinand's sex life.

The walk to school was very pleasant but the walk home was even better. A small stream followed the road for about a quarter of a mile. It was filled with animal life. I spent hours catching crayfish, called crawdads by the local populace and shuffling around barefooted trying to keep the crawdads from nipping at my toes. I learned their ways by observing them in their little castles and how they ate and lived. Sometimes I followed the stream as it left the road. About a half mile away it turned into a beautiful waterfall that dropped about 20 feet. It was a wild and wonderful place with no humans to intrude on the solitude of the quiet scene.

At home I amused myself with whatever books I could lay my hands on and with listening to Tom Mix on the radio whenever I could. One of the little girls in the neighborhood had a few bantam chickens as pets. They were called banty hens by the locals. We used to pick the docile hens up and place them on the nearest wire fence where they would amuse us by rocking back and forth in order to maintain their balance. We also caught horned toads vying in the challenge of picking them up before they could catch your hands on their "horns". Life was simple then.

I had another dog in Texas. I don't remember where we got him from but a dog was always part of my life. He was a good dog but he had this problem; he liked to chase and kill the neighbor's chickens. I could overlook his faults but, unfortunately, the neighbors wouldn't. We tried everything we knew how to correct this fault but nothing worked. The neighbors complained. Something had to be done. The situation came to a head one day when my Dad was absent. My dog had killed a couple of chickens and was caught in the act of blissfully dismembering them and spitting the feathers into the wind. My Mom, in desperation, asked a neighbor man to administer corporal punishment to the dog.

In spite of my pleas and tears the neighbor caught my dog, placed a rope around his neck and beat him unmercifully while my Mother and I looked on in tears. The poor dog cried and screamed at the treatment not really knowing why he was being tortured. Finally I couldn't stand it any longer and, having warned the man once without any response, I picked up a length of two-by-four and walloped him with it. He swatted me with a huge paw and I flew a few feet. Undeterred I approached him once more. My buddy was in trouble and only a coward would stand by and watch him absorb more punishment. Mom finally saw the whole episode getting out of hand and called a halt to the beating. I collected my dog and we retired to lick our wounds.

I remember Texas for heat, Tom Mix on the radio, lots of church time, horned toads, pecan trees, little banty hens and lots of blowhard Texas kids who apparently hated Yankees. I was happy when we finally shook the dust of that state off of our shoes and headed north. I've never had much use for Texans since that time and the batch of Texan Presidents we have had recently hasn't done much to ameliorate that feeling.

My father finally finished the seminary and became a Baptist minister. He had formed an alliance with a smooth talking preacher from Michigan who had impressed my father with his organization in St. Johns, Michigan. The preacher's name was Lougheed and he reputedly had a church, a church school and a radio program all devoted to the work of the Lord. The plan was for the two ministers to open a new church in Flint, Michigan. No one ever explained why Preacher Lougheed didn't return to his church in St. Johns or why he left it in the first place to attend the seminary in Ft. Worth, Texas. It was not my place to question and if I had no one would have paid any attention to me. As usual I kept my mouth shut and went along with the program.

Chapter Three

We arrived in Flint towing all of our earthly possessions in an old trailer. An old grocery store on Red Arrow Road in Flint seemed to be just made for the new church and initially my family took up residence in the back part of the store where the erstwhile grocer used to store his beer cases. There was a rudimentary toilet and small basin for ablutions but that was it. Undaunted we began the Lord's work by scrubbing the store and building a small podium and alter in one end. Folding chairs would serve the hoped for congregation until something better surfaced.

I was enrolled in a local school and, once again had to undergo the scrutiny and hazing of the ensconced populace of students who resented any intrusion into their territory. It mattered not one whit whether or not you were southern, northern, white, black or whatever. If you were a new kid you were prey, simple as that. I had to undergo the normal routine of fighting until everyone was satisfied with the pecking order. I knew it and they knew it. It was the normal order of things. After a few schoolyard batterings things would settle down. I really didn't matter who got battered, who won or who lost. What mattered the most was the spectacle and the excitement. We hadn't progressed all that far from imperial Rome. The lions were hungry.

My family progressed from the back of the grocery store-cum-church to an upstairs apartment of a neighbor. We finally were able to rent an apartment in an apartment complex two doors away from the church. Life began to take on a normal aura.

One of the neighborhood kids had his Grandfather living with his family. His "Grandpa" looked after him and participated in many activities with him. Grandpa built a wonderful "camp" for Jerry and any of his friends who were lucky enough to be invited into his circle of friends. The "camp" was a large hole in the sandy ground that had been covered with railroad ties, canvas and sand. The result was a room-sized abode that you had to enter by dropping down the "door", which was another hole in the ground. It was really very comfortable and had the added attraction of being out of sight of any adults or imagined enemies. Much later on in life I would encounter another abode much like this one. It would be the place where prisoners were kept in a POW camp run by the US Navy for pilots who had to undergo the school prior to being deployed overseas to areas that were unfriendly to our country. The school was called SERE for Survival, Escape, Resistance and Evasion. The place I had to sleep in was the mirror image of that nice camp that "Grandpa" had constructed.

A railroad spur ran behind the church and our apartment. Trains ran on it twice daily. We had the trains timed pretty well and would line nails on the rails which were crushed to amazing shapes by the engine. The engineer would always yell at us and threaten us in a vain attempt to shoo us away from the tracks. It never worked, of course. Trains were a definite attraction to bored young boys.

Hobos used to walk along the tracks. Our parents always warned us to stay away from those "dangerous people" but they seemed friendly enough and had many wild tales to tell if they were of a mind to talk to kids. One of them managed to talk Jerry into letting him sleep in the camp overnight. We thought that it was a humanitarian thing to do but the next morning the hobo was gone leaving in his stead an empty wine bottle and a large pile of human feces for several boys to bury. So much for the gratefulness of hobos.

School was OK here after things settled down. I had very few fights as I was a Yankee like everyone else as evidenced by my speech patterns although most of the kids thought that I had a strange accent. It wasn't strange enough to cause any turf wars however so I felt more or less at home even though I didn't know any of the kids.

Teachers were always intimidating. They all seemed aloof and unfriendly especially to a "new kid". All of them were female. One teacher even looked strange. She had no coloration at all. She was stark white and an unhealthy white at that. She also had a very intimidating manner about her. She was fond of giving little impromptu lectures about discipline in her class. I can almost remember, verbatim, her admonitions. "If you misbehave in my class you will be dealt with promptly. Biff-Bang, Bang-Biff. That's the way I treat unruly students." I made sure that I gave her no cause to "Biff-Bang" me. I witnessed her meting out her "discipline" to one small student one day. The teacher's hammering of the student resembled a street brawl rather than school discipline.

The street we lived on, named Red Arrow Road, was more or less in the country. A few blocks from my house there was an old abandoned apple orchard. The trees were ideal to climb and the apples were still edible. My friends and I spent hours in those trees eating apples and having wars by using them as ammunition. Most of my friends came from families with humble origins like mine and had few possessions just like me so we amused ourselves by exercising our wits. I think we had a more healthy childhood than most kids today who seem to lack for nothing but are bored most of the time anyway.

One day while we were climbing in the apple orchard a friend of mine named Wendell had a traumatic experience. Wendell was standing on a limb when it broke. He immediately and instinctively grabbed the limb over his head while he screamed for help. We gathered under Wendell shouting encouragement and trying to figure out how to assist him with his terrible predicament. A suggestion was made that we call the fire department. Wendell screamed that he couldn't hold on that long. It was several blocks to the nearest home and the fire department was miles away. We tried to talk him into hand walking over to the nearest large trunk. He shouted that he couldn't; he was afraid to let go with any hand in order to swing his body over for another handhold. He was bawling by this time and told us that he couldn't hold on much longer and that he was afraid of dying. That thought hadn't occurred to us prior to this and we began to be afraid also. I screwed up my courage and told him to let go and that I would catch him when he fell. That precipitated a scream of mixed rage and fear as he told me that I probably wasn't capable of doing that. I was indignant at his summation of my ability and a lively argument ensued.

Wendell became weaker and weaker but his screams became louder as the inevitable end drew near. Wendell was doomed to drop. There was no help for it. We had exhausted all possibilities and stood around with our mouths hanging open as we waited to witness Wendell's demise.

Suddenly with a loud wail Wendell let go and dropped, crashing to the ground. We all rushed over to see how he was and were relieved to find him sniveling and examining himself to see what was broken. Wendell had probably dropped all of eight feet. Nothing was broken and nothing was hurt. Wendell was a hero and that was that.

The circus was coming to town. It really wasn't a circus as much as it was a small carnival we called a "Carney". It was setting up in an open field not far from where we all played in the old apple orchard. We decided to watch the Carney people set up the tents. Three of us walked to the area and were busily engaged in open mouthed gawking at the sights when a tough-looking Carney woman saw us. "Hey, you", she yelled. "What the hell are you damned kids doing here. Get out of here."

Apparently we were a little slow to react. The Carney woman threw a bucket of some kind of liquid she was carrying all over one of my friends. I was fortunate enough to not be as close to her so I escaped dry but intimidated. We all ran as fast as we could to escape the wrath of this lady terror.

Preacher Lougheed had an adopted son named James. Naturally he was called Jimmy. Jimmy and I had established a close friendship, which was probably a natural thing since both of our fathers were co-preachers in the same church. In reality Preacher Lougheed

was the senior pastor since he had experience along those lines
and possessed squatter's rights. Accordingly he did most of the
preaching while Dad led the singing and the Sunday School. This set
of circumstances gave Jimmy seniority of a sort in the friendship.

Jimmy also had more experience in religious matters due to the
fact that his Dad had been involved in church matters longer. Being
Baptists, (I guess I was one due to the fact that my Dad was. I don't
recall ever being consulted in the matter but it wouldn't have made
any difference. I was from the era where children are to be seen and
not heard.). We didn't believe in "worldly things" such as dancing,
drinking, theatre or the movies. Jimmy imperiously had informed
me that his Dad had allowed him to see one movie to prove to him
how evil movies were. I believe the name of his movie was "Flying
Tigers". He reiterated, with great relish, how the pilots would get
shot in flight and how they would clasp their hands to their faces
while blood spurted from between clenched fingers. Jimmy was very
proud of having seen that "sinful" movie and loved to pontificate on
how absolutely wicked it was. I felt unfortunate at having not seen
the movie so that I could throw rocks at it also.

There was another factor that threw us together. You see, there
was this girl . . . . Her name was Adella and we both loved her deeply,
or thought that we did. We competed for her attention. I think she
loved the attention. What young girl wouldn't? There was never
any doubt in my mind concerning the outcome of all of this. After
all, wasn't I better looking, more intelligent, more daring and had a
better future than Jimmy? He wanted to become a preacher like his
Dad. I had absolutely no idea what I wanted to become but whatever
it was preaching had nothing to do with it at all. Additionally I also
had absolutely no idea about Adella or what she wanted as a future
companion or even if she wanted a future companion. Again, I had
no plans whatsoever concerning my future as regards something
called marriage. In all reality the term "plans" had not yet entered
my vocabulary. I had no plans for anything. Nada. My thoughts
concerning any outcome of the rivalry ended with the end of the
rivalry. The brave knight would win the fair maiden's scarf, end of
tale.

Jimmy never lost that aura of superciliousness whenever he was around me. That particular attitude was always embellished whenever the subject of Adella came up. To be truthful I don't know just why we were such good friends other than there simply weren't that many other kids around to chum around with. Inevitably the whole rub was bound to come to a head.

It started out quite innocently. Jimmy and I were tussling and wrestling on a grassy lawn. It began in fun but the rivalry flared up and neither boy wished to allow the other to get the upper hand. Holds became more painful; punches were thrown more in earnest. Both of our parents were sitting on a porch enjoying the sight of their boys engaged in a wrestling match. There were the usual catcalls and shouts of advice to one or the other of us. Suddenly I heard one of the adults say, "Wait a minute! They're really fighting." Both adult men rushed to break up the fight. When I recounted the various sins a Baptist could commit I forgot fighting. That was also proscribed.

Jimmy's father took charge and roughly, I thought, pulled us apart. He was holding us both by a shoulder. "What are you doing?" he asked his son.

"Well, he dug me," was the petulant reply Jimmy gave. The meaning here for the uninitiated who have never engaged in a street fight was that I had scratched him with my fingernails either advertently or by accident. That, in itself, was not surprising. Fingernails had the unfortunate ability to get in the way any time you attempted to grab anything. No self-respecting boy would ever try to scratch a foe. That was girl stuff, after all.

Preacher Lougheed shook me roughly. He leaned down and got right in my face. I was amazed to see so much hate and anger depicted on his visage. "Did you, Eddie?" he shouted. "Did you?" He punctuated each "Did you" with a shake.

I was angry to begin with. If Preacher Lougheed thought to cow me with his vindictives and shakes he was wrong. I clammed up and refused to speak. That gave Jimmy the ability to become the only witness to the crime. Later on, when I had a chance to study jurisprudence I became aware of the advantage I had handed him.

Since he was the only accuser and since I steadfastly refused to defend myself I was immediately adjudicated to be the guilty sinner. I was ordered to go to my room. I gladly obeyed just to get away from the sham of the whole incident. Jimmy was offered a soda and solicitous soothing and calming advice.

I believe this was the beginning of the breakup of the boyhood buddies. Sometime much later on in life I met with the same self-serving attitude on the part of people I thought of as "fellow travelers". They were always the people that you absolutely did not want as your friends. Sic semper the learning process.

Sometime after this incident Jimmy was trundled off to the same seminary our fathers had attended. I didn't miss him at all. In all fairness he was older than I was and at that age a few months can make a world of difference. I continued to live a happy carefree life and gave Jimmy not much thought at all. I was happy. There was no competition that I could see and Adella was all mine.

I thought.

I hadn't counted on the US mail and the fact that girls mature earlier than boys do. Looking back I now realize that Jimmy had never given up the ship. He continued to write to Adella and she apparently liked what he wrote. I was not aware that anything was wrong until much later when I received a letter from Adella informing me that she had chosen Jimmy and was going to be married to him.

The letter made a cold shiver run down my spine. Not because Adella had "chosen Jimmy" but because, up to this time, I had never even given a thought to a thing called marriage. Marriage? Marriage was for adults. I was still a kid. I thought like a kid and acted like a kid. I felt like a rabbit that had just escaped the farmer's trap. I couldn't believe that Adella had even contemplated marriage with me. I was still in school. I had no job. I didn't even know what I wanted to do with my life. The shiver returned. I would feel that same shiver later on, much later on, like when I almost crashed and was killed making carrier qualifications with the Navy in the Gulf of Mexico. That shiver was a conflict of emotions and feelings. On the one hand my body wanted to shut down. On the other my adrenalin system was operating at full bore and my body was fully geared in the flight or fight syndrome. Fortunately for me, in every instance the fight or flight syndrome always kicked in and I became a survivor.

I don't think that I ever answered Adella's letter. Most likely I felt that the trap was still set and waiting and I wasn't about to approach it again. I may be dumb but I wasn't a complete imbecile.

I got to see Jimmy again one more time. He had come home from the seminary at Christmas time and was an instant celebrity. He obviously ate all of the notoriety up and basked in the adoring light shining on him. I tried to rekindle the friendship but when I questioned a statement made by him he made a big deal of laughing (a laugh so obviously false it was pathetic) and saying, "Eddie has the temerity to term me a prevaricator". Now maybe he had a little more education than I had but this obvious "talking down" to everyone was belittling and patently elitist. Jimmy had just typed himself as far as I was concerned. I would never trust him again.

But I'm getting ahead of myself. Sometime later, after Dad had helped organize the little church on Red Arrow Drive he was offered a job preaching in a little church in St. Charles, Michigan.

Within a week or so we were on our way to the metropolis of St. Charles. The town was and still is a tiny village in the heart of farm country in central Michigan. The farmers there are solid German, Czech and Polish people who get up early, work hard and make very little money. They are the salt of the earth and have little time for hell, fire and thunder Southern Baptist preachers. Most of the people in the area were Catholic if they went to church at all. My father looked on the area as a target-rich environment. A more logical assessment would be that of a force-reconnaissance into enemy territory.

Dad found a rental house on an old farm outside of St. Charles. It was pretty primitive. It boasted an outdoor privy, one potbelly stove in the living room, a wood burning stove in the kitchen and a well that was accessed only from outside the house. There was no plumbing, hot or cold running water, toilet or central heating. It was primitive. It was an interesting way to live. The saving grace for the whole place as far as I was concerned was an old barn complete with barn rats and bales of hay. Another plus was a tiny "library" consisting of an enclosed bookcase filled with a variety of books. Before we had spent a year there I had read every book at least once.

The family who had lived in the house prior to our moving in had moved to a newer house about three miles away. They owned an old cat that considered our house as his house. Soon after the family moved away the cat disappeared from the new house and appeared at our back door. We first noticed him when my Mom heard a banging noise ensuing from the back door to a small enclosed "storm porch". The old cat knew how to open the door and was happily purring on top of a real icebox on the porch. Mom called the cat's owners and they picked him up the next day. He never really got the idea that he had actually moved. Either that or he was one stubborn cat. He repeated his hegira a number of times and each time he was kidnapped and taken back to his DP camp. I felt sorry for him but I was, like always, in the minority.

Now, about that icebox the old cat used to sleep on . . . . The country place where we lived was not served by an iceman. By this time refridgerators were rapidly replacing ice boxes. The job of an iceman was defunct. The farm we rented had no refridgerator. It was primitive. We existed on a subsistance level in that we only bought food that we could eat in the next two days. There was no refridgeration in the summer. In the winter we could put things like milk or meat in the small porch area that was unheated and that was our refridgerator. My family really existed in a time frame that was akin to what existed around the mid 1800s. it was an interesting life.

I've always thought that the various ethnic minorities were amusing. They cite case after case wherein they are discriminated against, put down, brow-beaten, used as slaves, not given opportunities to do whatever they wished, ignored, tortured and ill used. Various other minorities who are totally ignored and have no spokesmen can make the same claims. The minorities I speak of are the kids of Southern Baptist preachers, Mennonites, Amish and various other religious sects. Do you want to see slaves? Go to Lancaster County, Pennsylvania and talk to the Amish kids there, or the women. But it's all OK since it's in the name of God.

Black kids in the inner city? I've gone to school with them. They are not discriminated, put down, brow beaten, ill used, ignored, or tortured. Basically they simply do not wish to learn anything at all. They seem to be happy being what they are, unwashed, uneducated, unmotivated, unhappy and unemployed. Oh! And they revel in complaining about their lot at every opportunity.

Our farmhouse consisted of a large kitchen, a smaller living room and two bedrooms. The bedrooms were unheated and could get quite cold by early morning. The whole family would arise and dress either in the kitchen or the living room by the wood stoves there. Baths were conducted infrequently in the kitchen by the expedient of a large washtub filled with water pumped from the well outside and heated atop the stove in the kitchen. My parents had worked out a bathing schedule that was unknown to me. My sister and I had to use the same tub and water. She got to bathe first and I got the left over water. When we were finished the water was poured on the ground outside.

Everyone had to use the outdoor toilet. It was commonly called a "two-holer" and was smelly in the summer and cold in the winter. It possessed perks in the form of other life forms, namely spiders and hornets, all of which served to relax the person perched tentatively on one of the holes. I could never shake the idea of the whole structure collapsing and dumping me into the horrors residing below. An ancillary fear was that of a gigantic spider living underneath the seat just waiting for a chance to bite the large muscle that appeared irregularly to fill the hole. Needless to say, occasional bouts of constipation used to haunt me.

In actuality I was blessed by living by standards sort of how my Celtic ancestors, the Scots-Irish people lived. They would have viewed my circumstances as being very patrician but I thought of them as being very primitive. In perspective it's all in how one views their individual lifestyle. I lived no differently than thousands of kids in the poorer parts of the country lived. My Celtic ancestors were unwashed and dirty by modern standards. I lived in substandard conditions by modern standards. We all survived and were happy in our ignorance. The fly in the ointment is that once the scales are lifted from the eyes of the serfs they can never happily go back to their former conditions of existence.

No one wished to visit the outdoor privy at night. There were no lights wired up to the structure so anyone wishing to use it had to carry whatever sort of light they needed with them. Our family was relatively poor. Flashlights and battery powered lanterns were frivolous things that rich people possessed hence no one used the outdoor privy at night. An enameled steel chamber pot served for emergencies at night. It had a lid as a gesture toward sensitivity. It was my lot, as the junior serf in the clan, to empty the chamber pot each morning. I personally used it only for emergencies of an extreme nature hoping to set the example for its non-use but nothing seemed to work. Each morning found some offering within the hated pot and I had to carry it to the privy and empty it, washing it out under the pump after doing so. After washing the chamber pot I would empty it on the ground near the pump. It seemed the obvious thing to do. Much later on in life I would learn that a well collects any moisture that happens within an area cone that is subtended by a 45-degree angle from the well point to the surface of the ground. That means that the water I dumped out of the chamber pot eventually reached the well point and was, in theory anyway, served up on our table. The older I get and the more I know the more I am thankful for my ignorance earlier in life.

I attended school in the St. Charles Union School located in the heart of St. Charles. In order to get there I had to take the school bus every morning. The bus picked me up at a scheduled stop near the front of the farm in good weather but in the spring, fall and winter the dirt road we lived on was impassable and I had to trudge a half mile to the bus stop. The bus driver was an unpleasant man who seemed to blame me for having to drive down the poor road we lived on. His unpleasantness communicated itself to the other kids who rode the bus and a small, sour little girl took it on herself to make my life as unpleasant as possible.

I was used to, by this time, having to defend my honor in combat with whatever bully wished to take me on. A new kid always had to fight at least once whenever he attended a different school. I think that's written down somewhere as a law of nature or something like that. I was not about to subvert any such law so I was ever ready to fight and had the old radar going to see just who would challenge me. That I would be challenged was not in question. I knew it would happen. What I was totally unprepared for was to be challenged by a little girl. I could not attack her for two reasons. The first was an ethical one. I had been taught that you never, never, ever attack, hit or bother a female. To do so was almost a sin and Baptists hold sins very seriously. The second reason had to do with the manliness of the whole thing. Anything I did relative to the little girl would be wrong, cowardly and unforgivable. I was sandbagged. There was absolutely nothing I could do except stare straight ahead and allow the little terror to call me names, malign my manhood, ask embarrassing questions and harass me for the entire trip much to the amusement of the other passengers. I was fair game. I was the dog with the tin can tied to his tail that all of the other dogs were chasing. It was unfair war and I could do nothing about it. I suffered through two years of that without any end. The cretin bus driver seemed to enjoy the banter as much as anyone. To this day I've had no use for school bus drivers.

School itself was relatively pleasant. The teachers were old fashioned and very good at what they did. I think that I learned quite a lot at that school. The teacher used to read us the Laura Ingles Wilder books like "The Little House on the Prairie". I loved that series and always looked forward to the readings. Of course there was always the class clown to contend with.

There were very definite rules everyone had to contend with in class. One of them was an edict against chewing gum. I don't know why chewing gum was sinful. I didn't like it but I never saw any real reason for denying anyone else the privilege to chew whenever they wanted to but, once again, I was only a serf and had no say in the laws as propounded. The class clown saw things a mite differently and chewed whenever he wished. The teacher tried to whip him in shape by sitting him on a stool in front of the class with his chaw of chewing gum stuck on his nose. He loved it. He basked in the glory of being in the very eye of the class. When the class attention waned he proceeded to stretch his gum from his nose to his ears, then to his eyebrows and finally to his chin. He was a total mess by the time the teacher finally caught on to his game; that is to say, she saw what he was doing. I don't think she ever caught on to the fact that the clown only wanted attention. He would do anything for attention. Luckily he stuck to chewing gum to make his point.

As I've pointed out, most of the students of the Union School were farm kids. I count myself as one. This was in the 1940s and farm kids didn't bathe regularly. Once again I count myself as one of the unbathed. I used to get a bath about twice a week; that's a whole bath. I had to wash my face, hands and crotch every day, cold weather or not. Some kids didn't. A schoolroom full of unwashed bodies in the winter when the heat was on was an awesome thing to behold. Then there were some outstanding kids relative to the sense of smell. One of those kids was a large Polish or Russian girl named JoAnne. She was a good-looking girl and was pleasant but she had an aura that followed her around wherever she went. Kids playing tag would shout, "You've got Sherinski's fleas". I'm ashamed to admit that I shouted that right along with the rest. Another case in point was a boy named Duke who possessed the most god-awful breath anyone has ever witnessed. No one could stand near him and listen to him talk. One day a boy who was probably more attuned to things than the rest of us said, "I think we've all been giving JoAnne Sherinski a bad deal. Has anyone ever noticed that Duke's breathe smells like bullshit?"

Of course they had. The soapbox orator had a way with words. He further suggested that we give poor JoAnne a break and taunt with the challenge "You've got Duke's fleas". This last was a little more daring because the chances of Duke hearing the taunts and doing something about it were far greater than poor JoAnne doing anything about it, as big as she was.

The kids in school with me were like their parents, basic and the salt of the earth. Eddie Parletti was the son of the town's only tavern owner. I can remember that Eddie never seemed to have a warm coat in the wintertime and when he had somewhere to go that mandated his presence outside he used to run in order to minimize his outside presence. John Krawzak was a good friend and had a sense of humor like I had. We always could find something to laugh at. I remember one very cold winter we found a poor cat that had been kept outside and had frozen in someone's yard. The cat had died in a crouch with its head cocked to one side as if it were looking down a mouse hole. As kids are prone to do we used to throw snowballs at the pathetic little carcass all the while making jokes about the cat. I often wondered what came of those kids. Did they become farmers or did they go on to higher education and other things?

The best friend I had during this time was a large dog of uncertain lineage. The best guesses concerning his family tree was that he was the result of a Collie and German Shepherd love affair. He had come to me as a Christmas present from a friend of the family who owned a dairy farm in the area. The man and his family attended my father's church and we often ate Sunday dinner with them. I thought that the farm was a wonderful place and the farmer's dog, Corky, was even better. Corky was used to round up the cows and bring them to the barn each evening. All the farmer had to do was to tell Corky to "get the cows" and the dog was immediately off on his quest. I loved watching him work. The cows did not appreciate Corky's expertise, of course, and often would threaten him with their horns. The dog knew exactly how to handle that. He was much faster than the cows and would circle them, nipping at their heels. He never failed to bring the cows home.

One Christmas my father questioned me at great length concerning just what I wanted for a present that holiday. The answer was always the same. Corky.

We were invited to the farmer's home for Christmas dinner. I was delighted as it gave me the opportunity to see my friend. We had become fast friends and when not working Corky would follow me around and we would play endless games together. Dinner was superb and afterward I was surprised to see my buddy, Corky, walk through the kitchen and lay his head on my lap. This was a working farm and dogs were not allowed in the house. As I looked around to see if there was anything I could do to keep my friend from getting into trouble the adults all looked in on us and didn't seem all that upset at the spectacle of a large dog in the living room. The farmer, Mr. Kufeldt, smiled at me and said, "Look at his collar". Corky's collar had been replaced with a red ribbon and a tag that said, "Corky—To Eddie". I didn't understand at first so my Dad said, "I think he's your dog now". As realization hit me as to what had just transpired I threw my arms around the dog and hugged him. His tail was wagging so hard Dad said, "I think he'd better go outside now. He's about to wag lamps off of the tables."

I don't think I ever received a better Christmas present, ever, before or since.

Corky and I became inseparable. He had never known a leash and was a free agent. He would walk me to the school bus stop and wait until I boarded the bus. Then he would return home to attend to dog things until it was time for me to take the school bus home. Corky was always there when I got off of the bus. I never could figure out just how he knew when to meet me. He didn't own a watch and no one ever prompted him about the time. He was just there as if by magic. There were a few jealous kids on the bus who would make snide comments about my dog but nothing ever came of it as I ignored them and Corky looked too formidable to be trifled with. I always thought that the kids making the noise didn't have a wonderful dog like I did and were jealous.

Corky wasn't perfect by any means. Who among us are? The dog would wait for us whenever the whole family left in the car. He would wait by the mailbox until we came home and then, in a burst of happy exuberance he would leap the fence surrounding the neighbor's farm, joyfully round up the neighbor's cows and start them on a dead run for their barn before breaking off the attack and returning to us. Tail wagging he would look for praise, a nod or just a glance. Corky wasn't hard to please at all. I always made sure that he got a hug when we returned.

The neighbor didn't see things that way. He appeared more than once on our doorstep threatening my dog and even me if the "herding" syndrome didn't stop. He might have been successful if he had stuck to the facts but he became angry and started to threaten. He would have still been OK if he only threatened my dog as he was talking to Dad and Dad didn't view my dog in the same way that I did. Where the neighbor went astray was when he threatened me personally as the real "owner" of the dog. My Dad took threats seriously and they never failed to arouse his Scotch-Irish ire. He was a small man but not a person that you would want angry with you. I knew that first hand. The neighbor had to find that out the hard way. Dad told him that if he showed up again he would be very sorry and would probably have to undergo a convalescent period. The neighbor sniffed and allowed that my Dad's conduct was not in keeping with the best traditions of those espoused by the Southern Baptist Convention for preachers. That did it. After the tongue-lashing he received from Dad I don't believe he ever thought that he would really be welcome in Dad's church. We never saw him again. Dad figured that he had a lot of praying to do to ask for forgiveness for abusing his fellow man.

My father could be a terror when provoked. I always knew that but being only human I forgot from time to time and had to be reminded. Dad's unique way of reminding me was to have a heart-to-heart talk with me punctuated by the whip crack sounds of a heavy belt laid on my gluteal muscles. I always had to smile at the cartoon characters that told their sons prior to a spanking, "Son, this is going to hurt me more than it is you." Dad ever said anything like that and I'm sure that he never held that belief at all. Being a practical man he intended for corporal punishment to hurt and believe me, it did.

One day a small bitch in heat appeared on our lawn. Corky had never been "fixed", as the terminology goes and was a whole dog. Corky was delighted by the visit and did, as dogs down through countless ages are prone to do in like circumstances. Unfortunately for me my sister was in the area and, witnessing what Corky was doing she asked me, "What's Corky doing with that dog?"

Now although I was the town's preacher's son I was not isolated entirely from the local patois as spoken on farms in Central

Michigan. Accordingly and without giving my younger sister any lessons in sex education I told her, "Corky's just fucking that dog." End of conversation, I thought.

Suddenly there was an immense roar from the house and my father shot out of the door armed with the large, heavy belt I had become familiar with. He was making straight for me and I didn't have to glance around at all to see who his target was.

To gage the extent of Dad's anger you have to see things from his perspective. Here he is, studying his Biblical thesaurus, and his young daughter appears by his side to tell him, "Dad, you ought to go outside and watch Corky fucking a strange dog." Just imagine, the daughter of a straight-laced Southern Baptist preacher man who doesn't hold with smoking, drinking, carousing, dancing or really anything else, saying the awful "F" word to him. He instantaneously knew the source of this sin and reacted accordingly.

When my backside stopped smoking and I had a chance to assess the damage I determined never to say anything like that again in Dad's presence. Not only that but I had to watch for espionage agents who would report any intelligence gleaned to him.

We lived in an area of several dairy farms. Dad, who obviously had never heard about Louis Pasteur, had arranged to buy raw milk, fresh from the cow, from one of the farms that was about a mile and a half from our house. It was my task to wheel my old bicycle along the muddy, rutted road and gather two one-gallon jugs of milk from the farm and return home with them intact. I used the bike because it was helpful in carrying the heavy milk jugs. The road was barely passable by auto. It was impossible to ride a bike on it due to the dirt, ruts, mud and the shale scrap from a local coalmine used as a sort of covering in the attempt to make it more passable. I'll never forget the nights that I had to brave the winter snow and winds to make that trip after dark. Kids then were considered indestructible and were far more utilitarian than a gallon of gas.

In retrospect I am reminded of the Vietnamese peasants who used bicycles to transport goods and military ammunition over miles of jungle after we had interdicted their transportation routes. They beat us with primitive methods of transportation. I can relate to what it must have been to truck all of that stuff on bicycles over primitive roads.

One night during the summer Corky was wildly carrying on in the yard. Dad went out to see what was happening and returned quickly in a high state of excitement. "There's a possum in the tree out in front," he said. "Corky has it treed."

"Read," my Mom said, using my Dad's name, "call the dog in and it will probably go away."

"No, I'm going over to the neighbor's house and see if he has a shotgun I can borrow."

"Why do that? What are you planning on doing?"

"If I can get a shotgun we can have possum for dinner."

My Mom wasn't too happy to hear that. For one thing she wasn't all that sure that possum was something that civilized people ate. For another she was pretty sure that the job of skinning and butchering the little animal would fall in her lap. My father could not be dissuaded from his goal. He always thought that a good animal was one you could kill and eat. For him there simply wasn't any other criterion. Animals existed to be killed. The Bible says something like that. At least it says that God gave Man dominion over the animals of the earth. That was enough for Dad. That meant you could eat them. I always kept a weather eye on him. Who knew if he thought that dogs could be eaten or not? I knew from reading copies of National Geographic that some people somewhere on earth ate dogs. American Indians ate dogs. There was even a breed called "the Philippine Edible Dog". It was only a slight stretch from there to imagining my father eating my dog. Past history had shown my father's willingness to eat just about anything that moved. In moments of unkind thoughts concerning Dad I imagined him eating what cannibals called "long pig". The rest of the family didn't share his enthusiasm.

He was successful in borrowing a shotgun. I made sure that Corky was well away from the battle thinking that in some blood lust Dad might just include him in the perspective menu. Dad agreed that the dog should be kept out of the way as he didn't want to have to fight with Corky over possession of the dead body. Obviously the dog figured that he had squatter's rights over the possum since he had discovered the creature first. With Corky safely incarcerated in the barn protesting loudly I hurried into the house not wishing to view the execution.

We heard a loud bang followed by two more. Mom muttered something about "poor shot" and "we'll all break our teeth on the lead". Dad returned triumphantly stating that the deceased possum was in a washtub on the porch. He returned the shotgun to the farmer who probably had to clean it since Dad didn't own any tools for that purpose at that time. My thoughts were that it served the farmer right for having to clean the borrowed gun. He shouldn't have loaned it to an idiot anyway.

The next evening the possum was served as the main course. Dad tucked into it with gusto but the rest of the family ate vegetarian style all the while staring at Dad as if he were eating the family cat.

Easter was just around the corner. My sister and I both got baby ducks for the occasion. Mine was dyed blue and hers was pink. They were cute little rascals and we fell in love with them. They had names, of course, and were family pets. My sister and I fed and cared for them and they soon shed the colored feathers and became fine fat adults. Life was good and everything was wonderful until Christmas when my Dad announced that we were going to slaughter the pet ducks. There were protests, of course, that amounted to near mutiny but nothing could dissuade my carnivorous father from his prospective meal plans. I refused to participate but my father had other ideas concerning the whole activity. He thought that I was much too softhearted and needed a little hardening up. Accordingly I was told that I had to hold the ducks while my Dad chopped their heads off with a hatchet that he had found laying around in the barn.

Dad cheerfully sharpened the hatchet, whistling as he did. I thought that he was entirely too cheerful for an execution. He had an old stump all picked out as a makeshift guillotine. When the execution hour dawned I pleaded with him to allow me to abstain but he was adamant. I would participate as one of the executioners or would suffer corporal punishment. I should have stood my ground, accepted the punishment and made my protest meaningful. Instead, to my shame, I caved in and allowed my pet duck to go trustingly to the chopping block as I held him. I have since always deplored my cowardice.

Dad was never known for his grace and balance. He had me lay the duck's head on the stump. The duck was not cooperating at this time because he kept raising his head to look at me, probably wondering why I was crying. I kept talking to him and trying to get his head level with the stumps surface so his death would be instantaneous. As the military saying goes, "No good plan ever survives the first shot fired." Dad struck just as the duck moved his head. Instead of cutting the bird's head off the hatchet only hit him in the head cutting a deep groove into it. Blood spurted and the duck gave a great hiss as Dad continued to whale away with the hatchet. It took my ineffectual father three tries to dispatch my pet duck. I stuck around to make sure that no more torture would be applied and then called it quits. I informed my father that I would have no more to do with the rest of the celebration and he could try and whip me if he wished but if he tried I'd do my dead level best to stick the hatchet up his ass. I think my intensity got his attention. He allowed me to retire hors de combat.

Mom hadn't witnessed the murder of my pet duck and my sister was too young to know what was going on so everyone in my family ate roast duck for Christmas except me. I ate mashed potatoes and cranberry sauce. Anything else would have seemed sacrilegious.

That spring Corky found something else in our yard late in the evening. He was carrying on loudly as if desperately trying to tell us something strange was lurking there. Dad told me to find out why he was so upset. I went into the pitch-black yard and followed the sound of Corky's frantic barking. When I found him he was circling something and generally raising Cain. I approached him calling him to try and calm him down. As I neared the little animal Corky had cornered the little skunk figured that he had suffered enough insults and let go an accurate spray hitting his target squarely. Corky and I fled the scene a little too late. We opened the door to the house and were immediately denied access as if we had been diagnosed with advanced leprosy. Corky was banished to the barn where he lived for months in spite of the numerous baths I gave him. I had to strip naked, my clothes were buried and I had three baths prior to being allowed to retire for the night. Months later whenever my hair became wet I could smell the little skunk's lingering aura. In Corky's case it took years to finally get rid of the smell of skunk. Corky was adjudicated to be an outdoor dog for life plus one hundred years.

About this time my father found a house that had just become available to rent inside the town of St. Charles. After some dickering he announced that we would move there. Hallelujah. No more muddy roads and school busses. Indoor plumbing and water inside the house would be the new order of the day. I could walk to school and Dad would only be one block away from his church. Life was good.

There was one big detraction. Corky was not a city dog. He would cause many instances of head butting with neighbors who didn't appreciate his ardent militaristic attitudes toward cats and other dogs. He had to be chained up whenever he was not with me. He never really left my side whenever we wandered down by the Black River to fish with one of my new friends, a Chippewa Indian named Johnny. He was very protective and I loved it because I didn't have to fight any bullies whenever Corky was around. It only took one bite from him to convince any malefactors that it was better to leave us alone and look for easier prey. I didn't concern myself over feeling sorry for them. If they were so stupid to overlook Corky's withdrawn lips and the whites of his eyes then they deserved whatever they got. This was an age when the police and lawyers weren't consulted in minor matters like a bully getting bit while trying to harass some young boy.

Corky got so he would bark protectively whenever anyone walked by the house. He made a game out of it when he saw how startled they were. He would wait until they were at the closest point of approach and then dart out ferociously barking as if he were going to eat them as, indeed, they thought that to be the case. He always looked like he was smiling whenever they would yell and jump. I'm absolutely sure that he was bored and made a game out of it all. Regardless, game or not, he was not appreciated by many other people. He continued to be chained up whenever I was at school.

Much to my delight I found out that the town library was housed over the town fire station next door to our house. It wasn't much of a library as libraries go but it was a treasure trove as far as I was concerned. I made friends with the librarian, a little old lady who loved books as much as I did and did what she could to protect them from barbarians. She naturally categorized me as a barbarian because of my age. I would have to prove myself to her before she would completely trust me.

I produced all of the documents she required in order to check out a book. Once cleared I checked out the maximum number allowed. She was suspicious of me but absent any proof that I intended harm to the books in her charge she had no alternative but to let them go home with me. I read the books with a voracious appetite. It was summertime, school was out and I had nothing to do. Reading could wile away the hours and transport me to far away places and wonderful adventures.

When I checked the books back in the little librarian quizzed me about them. She wanted to know if I had really read them or not. I spent an hour or so talking to her and at the end of the conversation we were fast friends. She discovered that I loved books as much as she did and that I had an unquenchable appetite for knowledge, new things and new ideas. She was also pretty lonely. The small library in a farming town is not well attended and I suspect that there were days when the library spaces didn't see even one patron. It got so that I would visit her at least once each day. We would discuss books in general and some specific titles. She always alerted me about any new titles that would be received by the library. I think that I was the first person in town to read <u>The Yearling</u> when it came out.

Weekends were a problem. The maximum number of books any one person could check out at any one time was three. I could easily go through three books before the end of the day on Sunday, depending on the books. Real fear was not having any books to read. I confided my concerns to the librarian and she broke the rules for me. She said that she could see no reason why I couldn't check out as many books as I wished, within reason, of course. I was ecstatic. I no linger had to fear boredom on Sundays after church.

An aside is in order here. I said, a few sentences prior to this, that real fear was not having any books to read. I've never lost that fear. Many years later when I was the Captain on a Northwest Airlines 747 I used to carry several unread books on my trips to Southeast Asia. The trips were usually around twelve days long with long layovers in such exotic places like Singapore, Kuala Lumpur, Hong Kong, Bangkok, Manila, Tokyo and, well, you get the picture. Due to the large time changes sometimes I would find myself wide awake at two o'clock in the morning with absolutely nothing open and nothing to do to amuse myself. At times like those the ability to immerse myself in a tub of hot water and read a good book was priceless. I always felt sorry for those pilots who had never cultivated a burning desire to read.

Corky was lost because of my discovery of the library. Prior to finding the library I used to spend hours wandering around with my dog. Now he remained tied up in the back yard while I read in the house. When I finally discovered that my old friend was lonesome I started reading on the back porch so he could lie at my feet and put his head in my lap. As long as I did that he was happy.

I think that I learned more that summer reading than I did all through the school year in regimented studies.

All good things must come to an end. Summer waned and it was time to go back to school. The Catholic kids went to the parochial school in St. Charles so they were effectively isolated from the rest of us. Nevertheless I made friends with two brothers who lived a couple of blocks away. When one of them had a birthday I was invited to his party. I was, I think, the only Protestant kid who attended the party. I knew no one there and was an outsider. I stood around silently looking on as everyone else had fun. They all seemed to know each other. Not surprising since they all attended the same school. I was pointedly ignored right up to the time when the inevitable challenge came to do battle with one of the revelers. He said that he wanted to know how tough a Protestant kid was. I lasted through the first blow and left. My heart wasn't in it. I was in strange territory and knew it.

This was not so far removed from going to a new school. The same rules applied. It was always necessary to beat up on the new kid. Must have been a law or something as far as I was concerned. I went home to my dog and my books.

That winter it was unseasonably cold. The Black River that flowed through St. Charles froze over early and made all of the ice fishermen happy. Mr. Kufeldt, the farmer who had given me Corky, owned an ice-fishing house on skids that he loaded onto a pickup truck and drove to the river. He invited my Dad and I to a day of fishing with him.

The river was frozen so well that cars could drive on it. Dad drove our car along about a mile of river ice until we saw Kufeldt's ice shanty. He parked the car alongside the shanty and we went into a whole new world inside the structure. Inside it was warm and dark. Mr. Kufeldt had a small space heater set up inside the shanty that was more than adequate to heat the small space. Several stools inside surrounded a large rectangular hole cut into the ice. The sun shining on the river ice made it seem as if we were standing on the top of the water with the ability to see clear to the bottom of the river. Several small artificial baitfish were suspended in the water on wires. Mr. Kufeldt would agitate the wires every once in a while to make the lures seem alive. Occasionally large fish like Pike would investigate the lures. If they were considered a fish that Mr. Kufeldt wanted to keep he would spear them. The fishing was selective and efficient. No fish was harmed if it wasn't wanted for dinner. Meanwhile I sat in warm reverie watching a parade of fish swim by. It was magical.

We visited Mr. Kufeldt's shanty several times that winter. Finally Dad announced that he thought that it wasn't safe to venture out on the ice any longer. Mr. Kufeldt thought so too as he moved his shanty onto dry ground. Others were of a different opinion and kept on fishing until one of them lost his car as it broke through the river ice and ended up setting on the bottom with 15 feet of water on top of it. That effectively ended the fishing season. I always thought that the incident was a very classy way to end the year's ice-fishing season.

The little church that Dad led was tiny. It probably had somewhere around twenty or thirty members at any one time. Other people would be persuaded to attend for a few weeks from time to time but Dad was working against the wind. His environment consisted of mostly catholic Polish and Czechoslovakian farmers. They didn't think too much of religion in general and a Baptist was a strange animal to them, one to be avoided. Still the little church persisted in spite of the overwhelming odds. It would never pay for a real full-time pastor. The best it could ever hope for was to have a part time one, perhaps one that had a regular full-time job outside of the church. It was quaint. One of the "regulars" would always ring the bell in the church's steeple. Often I would be called upon to help him as he was aged and appreciated a young body to pull the bell chain. There were precious few young folk to chum around with. I can remember only one. He had the most awful voice I've ever witnessed when it came time to sing the hymns that were listed to be sung that Sunday.

The regular people who attended the little church were of the same type that populated the little village of St. Charles. They were basic, salt of the earth folk. When hymns were sung, often with no one to play the piano, it was cacophony. In one of the psalms in the Bible it says, "Make a joyful noise unto the Lord, all ye lands". The most you could say concerning the hymns being sung were that they were joyful. When the congregation sang "Bringing in the Sheaves" a little old lady near me sang "Bringing in the sheeps". No one had the courage or the meanness to tell her the difference.

There were absolutely no females my age in the whole church. Dad continued to trudge along witnessing to his tiny flock and exhorting them to better lives. As far as I could see most of them lived exemplary lives and I could see no way that they could better themselves in any way. That didn't deter Dad in the least. He continued to harangue the little congregation while they stoically sat in the pews and took the abuse without comment.

One day Dad was visited by a delegation of people from his old church; the one on Red Arrow Road. They had some squabble among themselves and for some reason thought it advisable to bring my Dad into the argument. Things got out of hand and there was a lot of shouting. The delegation went away vowing revenge of some sort and shortly after that my Dad got discouraged with his church in St. Charles. Dad could never divorce himself entirely from the shortcomings of his congregation. He could never quite figure out that there never had been a perfect congregation or a perfect human being. He took all shortcomings, backslidings, sins and foibles as a direct slap in the face. Everything was his fault, or so he thought. He became more and more morose and gloomy. As he did so he lost more and more people in the church who simply didn't enjoy being around him any more. Who wants a steady diet of a recounting of their sins and constant exhortations to reform? The church finally got so tiny that it simply imploded and there was no one left to preach to. Dad decided that St. Charles didn't deserve him any longer and we moved back to Flint, Michigan.

Chapter Four

$\mathcal{D}$ ad decided to become a house painter instead of a preacher. It seemed to be a workable idea, as he had never made much money as a small town preacher. Word got around that he was a good painter and soon he had enough work to keep him busy full time. He seemed happier now that the sins of the world were lifted from his shoulders. I know that his family was much happier.

We lived in a small area of Flint called "Thrift City", a workingman's neighborhood of solid, down to earth people. Dad rented a small house, just big enough for the four of us. As luck would have it I had just entered junior high school and began my continuing education at Lowell Junior High. I didn't know it at the time but Lowell was known as a "tough" school being about equally divided between black and white students.

I had not attended a school since leaving Texas that had any black kids enrolled in them. St. Charles had no black citizens. All of a sudden I seemed inundated with them. Being rather stupid and naïve where the social graces were concerned I completely forgot the lesson learned in kindergarten relative to a certain ethnic minority group.

On my first day at the new school I had the pleasure of attending a gym class with the usual mix of black and white kids. The gym teacher thought to break the ice by having the entire class play a game of tag ball. The class was divided up into two equal parts and the ball was launched. One side would fire the ball at the other side.

Whomever it hit was "out" of the game. The black kids thoroughly enjoyed the game and would run screaming across the gym floor. I had never witnessed any male scream in a high falsetto before this and laughingly yelled, "Listen to those niggers scream!"

I was immediately branded either extremely tough or very crazy by the kids who had lived in the area for some time and who knew how the black kids thought and what they were capable of. Suddenly there was a large vacant area around me as others sought to get as far away from me as possible in order to avoid the certain wrath that was bound to descend upon me. Luckily if any black kids heard me they must have thought that I had to be tough enough not to care about what I said and deemed it advisable to ignore me. Most likely the factor that prevented me from being hammered on the spot was that the kids were making so much noise they didn't hear me. At any rate people walked softly around me for some time thinking perhaps that I was an unknown entity, a loose cannon, a time bomb waiting to explode.

My education at Lowell was two-fold. On the one hand I learned what every other kid learns in Junior high school; English, history, science, math, etc. On the other hand I learned the very practical aspects of how to get along with a sizeable black minority in close proximity to me. The former was easy. The latter was very hard.

Most of the male black kids seemed not to care at all if they got any education or not. A sizeable group of the female black kids felt the same way. Most of the black kids were friendly but sometimes unpredictable depending on the topics of conversation they had been subjected to the night before. They could be sullen and, at times like those, were best avoided. They were earthy in the extreme; my vocabulary grew by leaps and bounds at Lowell but the words and phrases I learned were never to be used around my family. I learned that you could start a fight just by saying "Yo' Mama". Most of the kids amused themselves by reciting a series of short poems aimed at denigrating some other kid. This was called, "playin' the dozens". I never did figure out the meaning of "the dozens", I just accepted the name like everyone else.

A sampling of "playin' the dozens" is, "I don' play the dozens, I plays the fo's an' fives. I gets yo' Mammy when yo' Daddy dies". I'll leave it up to the reader to interpret the ditty. It seemed that any reference to one's maternal parentage was a cause to do battle.

The black kids were very concerned and open with sexual matters. The boys were always grabbing at their crotches and pulling on their genitals. They also very overtly grabbed at the black girls breasts and crotches. Uptight white kids found this embarrassing. Black kids found the white kid's embarrassment humorous. Most of the male teachers of that time owned large wooden paddles much like the modern day fraternity paddle. They used these paddles to maintain order in an otherwise disorderly classroom. Female teachers, when provoked, would appeal to a male teacher who would, without hesitation, lean a miscreant over and wallop him once or twice with his paddle. Some kids were paddled almost daily.

The drill would go like this. "You! Yeah, I mean you! Get up here!" The sinner would move to the front of the room grinning at his buddies and holding his posterior as if he had already been paddled. The teacher would bend him over in a stance like you would adopt if you wished to touch your toes. The rest of the class would howl, "Oooouuu" in enjoyment. Usually the teacher would fake hitting the prisoner who would always try to time the blow by straightening up at the exact moment the paddle landed in order to soften the pain. The teacher, used to this ploy, would set up a metronome of fake swats until he had the sinner out of sequence or synchronization. At that time the paddle would land. Smack! The teacher always won. Howls of triumph would ring out from the massed class as the chastened kid would make his way back to his seat rubbing his sore posterior. It was bedlam, squared. The number of "swats" was left entirely up to the discretion of the teacher and depended on the transgression of the sinner.

Not all corporal punishments were based on the ubiquitous paddle. Sometimes the teachers were forced to improvise. In the 1940s teachers were always given the benefit of the doubt when it came to corporal punishment. Usually, unless the bloodletting was excessive, nothing was ever even mentioned regarding the punishments meted out to the sinners. Normally the sinners in question knew, without a doubt, that they had transgressed beyond the ability of the longsuffering teacher to ignore them. Those teachers who possessed a "short fuse" when it came to classroom discipline were well known and those classrooms were normally very well behaved and peaceful.

One such teacher was Mr. McGhan. He was built and looked like an English bulldog. Prudent people, upon seeing such a sight, would have behaved themselves in an exemplary manner. Kids in junior high school are generally not prudent. It usually takes a very strong empirical example to force lessons into young minds. In Mr. McGhan's case he did an admirable job of showing the flag.

Mr. McGhan taught mathematics. He was a perfectionist and tended to look down on those who seemed to express little interest in the discipline. One day he saw, to his amazement, that one of his male subjects had actually fallen asleep during a lengthy discourse on one of the more involved explanations concerning a problem that he had placed on the board. Not only had the sinner fallen asleep but he was also seated in the front row of desks directly in front of the teacher. Again, not a prudent thing to do.

Mr. McGhan gave the sinner every chance to account for himself. The teacher stooped down and peered at the student in a careful manner. The silence in the class was pregnant. The student was hors combat and had even begun to snore. That was the straw that sank the boat.

Mr. McGhan's eyes and mouth both opened wide. He gave a marvelous roar that woke up the rest of the class. Then he kicked the bottom of the snoring student's desk making the whole desk with the student intact turn a flip and land upside-down. It was better than watching a circus act. The student was disoriented, to say the least and this prompted a chorus of laughter from the other sinners in the class who were thankful that he had been apprehended and not them. The student, once he had extricated himself from the desk, was summarily banished to the dean's office. The only thing that came of the incident was that most of the students tried manfully to stay awake in Mr. McGhan's class.

Another student fancied himself the class clown. He clowned around in every class that he attended. Unfortunately he tried his act in a class that tried to teach kids machine drawing, an offshoot of drafting classes and an exacting offshoot at that. The class was serious business. Clowning was not listed in the curriculum. Of course the teacher became almost immediately aware of this transgression. He silently walked over and stood next to the kid. He carried a three cornered ruler in his hand. Actually the ruler was held in both hands and his knuckles were white, clear evidence of the tension being built up in those hands. I had always considered the kid to be rather stupid and this time he proved that I had been correct. He continued to clown around, giggling and pointing at the teacher standing near him. Suddenly the teacher reached his limit of tolerance for fools and released one end of the ruler with one hand. The ruler flipped over and impacted the kid's head in a distinct "whack". I thought, "Damn! That had to hurt". The kid doubled up holding his head with both hands. The teacher shouted, "Out! Get out!" The kid was happy to go. He reported to the Dean's office and was given more punishment. Nothing happened to the teacher. Discipline was enforced in that school in the 40s and the kids were better for it. Today's kids are free to curse teachers and ignore discipline and learning. Nothing can be done to them to enforce discipline. Which school do you, the reader, think was the more effective?

Some of the black kids had flunked school enough to be much older than the rest of their class. During the 1940s it was quite acceptable to flunk a kid if he did not perform. No one cared if it hurt his feelings or "damaged his self image". The older kids were more muscular and more fleshed out than the rest of the class and could easily bully and push any of the smaller kids around. These flunkouts were king of the heap. Some could be quite dangerous.

One afternoon the gym teacher, a Mr. Don Jones, ex-Marine, happened to be walking through the school corridor after the school had been dismissed. Several of the bigger black kids were loitering in the hall against school policy. Mr. Jones casually called out to them and told them to leave the school unless they had business there and could prove it. An argument ensued, the kids complaining that Mr. Jones had no right to kick them out of their school. I was walking down the same corridor and stopped to see what was happening.

Normally no one would challenge Mr. Jones. He was low key and tough. When he said something people usually listened. This was not the case this time. One of the bigger black kids challenged the gym teacher and pulled a sharpened garden trowel from his back pocket saying, "You Mutha-fuk. I goin' to cut yo' ass." Sharpened garden trowels were the weapon of choice among a certain segment of kids. They were an effective weapon, they fit the pocket perfectly and, in a pinch, could arguably be claimed to be just what they were supposed to be, a garden trowel.

Mr. Jones usually began the class year with a demonstration. When the class assembled in the gym they would find the teacher sitting on the floor underneath a long piece of rope fastened to the ceiling. (Sailors would classify this as "line" but I digress.) Without a word the teacher would proceed to climb the rope, hand over hand, with his legs still held at a right angle to his body as if he were still sitting on the floor. He would climb until he could touch the ceiling and then, legs still held at that 90-degree angle, would descend slowly until he was sitting on the floor once more. He never had to say a word. The class understood the implied message all too well. Apparently the kid challenging him this day had been absent for the demonstration.

Did I say that Mr. Jones was an ex-Marine? In all reality there is no such animal. Once a Marine, always a Marine. I didn't know this at the time but I learned it much later in life. It made complete sense in retrospect.

Mr. Jones calmly removed his glasses and handed them to one of the kids watching him saying, "Would you hold these for me please?" He then leisurely stepped forward and kicked the hand holding the garden trowel sending the trowel flying. While the kid who had threatened him was still wondering what was happening Mr. Jones kept up the advance hitting him with a short chop to the chin that completely KO'd the kid. As the kid started to drop Mr. Jones grabbed one of his arms and, turning his body, he threw his opponent over his shoulder in a perfectly executed Seio-Nagi Judo throw. The black kid went headfirst into a line of lockers with a sound like a dinner gong at a Chinese supper. He laid there looking like a rumpled bunch of rags. Mr. Jones wasn't even breathing hard. He reached for his glasses, thanked the holder for helping him, grabbed a fistful of shirt on the unconscious sinner and dragged him to the Dean's office. The corridor was suddenly and silently vacated.

Mr. Jones was my first introduction to a Marine when I didn't even know what a Marine was. I was favorably impressed and still am. I was suffused with a desire to do whatever Mr. Jones wished done. I didn't know why. Later on I would learn that it was due to a nebulous attribute called leadership. Mr. Jones was a very self-assured leader and didn't need anyone to point that attribute out to him. People simply wanted to do what Mr. Jones wanted them to do. It was magic.

Another perpetual flunkout was a black kid named Tyson. Kid is actually a misnomer; this kid was still in the 7th grade and was worried about the draft into the military, which was still in effect in the 1947 era. I never knew if Tyson was a first or last name. He was only known as Tyson. Tyson always had a fey look about him as if he were listening to someone or something that no one else could hear. His eyes would wander up and to the right whenever he talked to you, which was seldom. Usually he would just smile and let his tongue hang out. Most of the kids would only communicate with him by yelling, "Hey, Tyson, hit a lick." At that Tyson would tap-dance until you said, "Stop". He had an after-school job like a lot of the other kids during that period only instead of a paper route or working in a grocery store he was employed in a whore house on Michigan Avenue, the red light district in Flint at that time. Tyson's job involved picking the pockets of the jons who were engaged in sexual activity and therefore not too observant. Usually the jon's trousers would be hanging on a chair strategically placed near a door. Tyson was interesting to say the least. He was interested in a female teacher, the youngest, prettiest teacher in the whole school. He used to do things in order to be ordered to stay after school. He would then stare at her and leer; obviously engaging in flights of fancy that involved her. I always thought that she must have been either pretty naïve or pretty dumb in order to keep that guy after school.

The Science class was the worst of the lot. It was run (not taught) by an old man we all called "Baldy" Anderson. I think he was senile. He was oblivious to anything the black kids did but would leap on any imagined fault of a white kid and punish them for it. After seeing one tall black kid named Emmitt Marsh masturbating in public in the back of the class egged on by the hoots of his friends culminating in an ejaculation into one of the drawers in the tables we had to use, I determined not to use any of the desk drawers in that particular class. I also determined never to let old Baldy to malign me. I went to war with him. I got kicked out of his class several times and had to go to the Dean's office. The Dean couldn't figure it out. I never had any trouble with anyone else and always got good grades. Finally the Dean called my Mom and she embarrassed the hell out of me by accompanying me to the class one day. Envision, if you will, your Mother accompanying you in a class in junior high school. I was humiliated. I would forever be the butt of any jokes about "yo mamma havin' ta stick up fo' yo". She saw first hand what was going on in the class and after a talk with the Dean, Baldy was on a short leash leading to retirement. Baldy always liked to teach the class artificial respiration. The state of the art at that time was for the person doing the respiration to position himself atop the prone victim facing in the same direction and to roll his weight onto his arms with his hands placed on the victim's ribcage. Baldy would intone, "In goes the good air, out goes the bad air," in time with the respiration attempts. Baldy always chose two black kids for a demonstration. As a normal thing the kid doing the respirations would leer at the class and mime pelvic thrusts on the "victim" who would then arise from the dead and, holding his posterior, would parade around the class demanding to know, "Who felt my ass?" In a more enlightened country those kids would have been pressed for oil or hired out on peanut farms.

Steve Evanish was a sly kid who really didn't belong in an institution of learning. He constantly got into trouble because he was too stupid to duck. He had no use for education but attended school because he had to. Steve made the mistake one day of threatening me with a fish-filleting knife. I took the knife away from him by kicking his hand much like I had seen Mr. Jones do with the kid who threatened him. Then I beat the crap out of him and kept his knife. Steve was no contest and I didn't like the idea of being cut.

Steve got into trouble one day by becoming angry with some black kids and calling them niggers. They easily ran him down and threw him into a hole in the ground that contained some pumps for the school. After they slammed the cover on the hole they all lined up and urinated on the cover. I'll never forget the sight of good old Steve setting there with pee dripping off of his nose. At least he had the good grace to go home after that instead of going back to school.

Everybody carried a knife at Lowell. It seemed to be part of the uniform of the day. I was no exception. I carried two; just in case. Every spring rumors surfaced that a race riot would ensue. All of the kids in the metal shop class made weapons, just like in prison. Everyone was armed, even the girls. Some of the so-called weapons were laughable but others were deadly. The school seemed oblivious to the whole issue, which usually died down after a few forays.

I hated the shop classes. Since this was a blue-collar area school shop classes were popular. I had to attend a wood shop and a metal shop class. I had no choice as there simply wasn't anything else to take to round out the school day. The metal shop class was bad. I hated the craft anyway and it was run much like the automotive shops that were ubiquitous in the Flint area. Each shop class had to have a "foreman" who would operate under the teacher. The job of "foreman" was a democratically chosen position. I guess it was assumed that the democratic process was an attempt to teach the young barbarians something. It taught some things all right.

The class I attended had two people up for a vote, a black kid and a white kid. The white kid stumped by making a little speech telling everyone why he thought he would make a good foreman. The black kid dispatched a few friends who would stick the point of their knives into your side and mutter, "You goin' to vote for Lewis, ain't ya?" He would back off if you nodded. The rub came because the ignorant savages didn't figure on a secret ballot so when the white kid won they couldn't exactly figure whom to punish. I'm sure the whole process was a harbinger of things to come in their future. The goon squad would never really figure out how things worked and would probably end up in the prison system sometime anyway.

I had always been aware of a stubborn streak in my persona. I usually was able to downplay it because it would mostly come to the fore when my Dad wanted something and I learned early on not to try and make an end run around him. With peers it was different.

One day I was playing football with a few friends. We really weren't playing football per se but were passing the ball around. Some bigger kids wanted the ball and told us to give it up. I mouthed off and told them that it was ours and to leave us alone. Thus singled out they assumed that I was the spokesman for the group and one of the biggest kids approached me telling me, "OK, smart guy. Give me the ball".

"Go to hell," was the response as I hid the ball behind my back.

"C'mon, kid, give me the ball or I'll beat your ass."

"Fuck you."

He grabbed me and tucked my head under his arm. Holding me by my hair with my head under his arm he demanded the ball one more time. I was struggling and cursing him. Finally he hit me in the face with his fist. Blood spurted and by now I was crying with rage and frustration. The more I cried the madder I got. Crying was for kids and sissies. I was neither. I raged at the bigger kid. Snot and blood dripped from my mouth and nose. He kept repeating his demands and I kept telling him to go perform a sexual impossibility on himself. Each time I did so he would hit me.

Finally one of his friends became alarmed at the amount of punishment I was absorbing. "Hey, Jerry, let the kid go. You're going to kill him."

"Damn right I am if he doesn't shut his mouth."

"Fuck you, asshole". Slam! Once again, right on the nose.

Finally the bigger kid gave up. He allowed as how he would let me go for my own good but I'd never better do that again. As he left I gave him one more "fuck you". He shook his head and departed with the ball and I went home. I was a mess. Dad looked me over and asked how the other guy faired. I told him of the moot fight and he just shook his head. At least I wasn't taken to task for cutting school that afternoon.

I walked to school each day. It was about a mile but I had plenty of company so it was OK. I had made close friends with an American Indian kid named Tom. He had come to Lowell from another school and needed a friend. I filled the bill. Tom was a buddy. We joined a Boy Scout troop together and would remain in the Scout program for years. We had to cross a system of railroad tracks in order to get to the school and an opportunity for adventure arose. I found that you could run alongside of the train and hop onto one of the short ladders leading to the top of the cars if you were careful. From there you could climb on top of the car and run along the whole length of the train. You could even climb down the rearmost ladder onto the caboose and activate the shrill whistle at the rear of the caboose. It was exciting, heady fun and always upset the engineer. Ever so often a railroad cop would chase us but that only gave more excitement to the fun. Sometimes the engineer would see us and speed up in a vain attempt to dissuade us but we were pretty resourceful and found that we could hop just about any train that would navigate through the switching yard. Besides, speeding up in a train was a non sequitur. Big things such as trains cannot speed up fast enough to prevent even garden snails to hitch rides. It was more fun than throwing some dumb ball around.

I had a job after school in a small grocery store. It was illegal since I was too young to hold a job in the State of Michigan but the storeowner liked the way I worked so he ignored the statutes. One day a man entered the store and asked for the owner. He was dressed in rough clothing but flashed a badge that got everyone's attention. He wanted to talk to a boy named Eddie Landers. The storeowner almost swallowed his tongue. The penalties for illegally employing a minor were harsh and the fines were heavy. He managed to point at me and the railroad cop walked over and had a heart-to-heart talk with me. He had found my Dad first and Dad told him where to find me. Dad said for him to scare the hell out of me. He did exactly that and in the process scared the hell out of the storeowner. I was caught fair and square and confessed immediately. The cop was nice and after chewing me out he made me promise never to fool around with trains again. Fair was fair and I promised. I kept the promise and counted myself as lucky. I did lose my job, however. The storeowner figured that even as good an employee as I was it wasn't worth the coronary I would certainly give him sooner or later.

Corky had to be tied up more and more. He became more irate as time went on and would beat up on any other dogs he could catch. Finally Dad told me that he had to go and that Dad had found a family who lived in the country who had two young girls who would love and cherish Corky. I had no choice in the matter once again so I had to part company with my old buddy. It was a tearful parting. I mourned for a week but one day as I opened the door there stood my buddy, happily panting and wagging that wonderful tail. He had run away from the farm, which was a long way away and had found me. I was ecstatic but Dad told me he couldn't stay so once again we took him back to the farm. This time the family promised to keep him tied up until he had forgotten me. I'd like to think that he was happy there. I never saw him again.

I moped around for a while mourning my lost dog. One day an old man who ran one of the corner grocery stores gave me a tiny pup of uncertain parentage. He was christened Ted and became my new buddy. He was a small dog and wasn't any real trouble in that he was friendly to both humans and animals. He lived on an enclosed back porch where Corky had lived. I took care of him and when he got a terrible cold I dosed him with Vick's Vaporub as my

Dad didn't see any merit in taking a dog to the doctor. The poor dog hated the Vick's but somehow he got over his illness. Mom thought that he was going to die so I guess we were all lucky. I never found out if the Vic's helped or not but it was the only prescription I could come up with, limited as I was in Materia Medica.

As a Baptist preacher my Dad had lots of friends who specialized in religious things and attitudes. One family in particular impressed me in such a way that they still are in the forefront of my memory. They were such excellent Christians that they hovered over the television set in their living room and whenever any advertisements appeared that had anything to do with the sinful things like cigarettes, movies, dancing or anything else that smacked of worldly pleasures that were proscribed by the Baptist congregation they would leap on the TV and turn it off. They would then observe the time carefully so as to turn the set back on just as the program returned. It was distracting to say the least but it showed any visitors the scope of Christianity the family possessed. I observed the proceedings with a jaundiced eye.

The two boys who belonged to this most Christian of families were the targets of this protective service. They said all the correct things and showed the flag any time it was required to do so but they were kids just like all kids. One day when we were all alone, that is to say sans adults, the subject of sex reared its ugly head. The older of the two boys made the observation that everybody "did IT". An immediate argument ensured between the two boys. The younger of the boys was a purist and believed that only bad people "did IT". The older, wiser boy argued in vain in order to prove his point and at some time made the horrible observation that; "Dad did "IT" to Mom. How do you think you got here?"

The younger boy was horrified at that enlightened remark and screamed, "Mom did not!" That prompted the argument from the brother, "She did too. So will you when you grow up. You'll have to!"

That did it. The younger brother was in tears when he vowed that he would never, never do such a wicked and dirty thing. His brother was unrelenting when he yelled, "Yes you will. You'll have to." The little guy fled before any more foul words could sully his ears. I congratulated myself on not laughing during the whole dialog.

Like a lot of young boys I figured that I knew a lot more than I actually did. One day a group of boys got into a discussion about sex. What else was there to really talk about in junior high school? One of the boys was educated on the subject. His parents had taken the effort to talk to him about the birds and bees early on. The rest of us were abysmally ignorant. The discussion eventually centered on childbirth. An immediate argument ensued as to exactly where the newborn exited the mother's body. The more knowledgeable kid swore that the child exited via the woman's vagina. I knew better. I argued that it came out of her anus. Of course we didn't use the technical terms like vagina and anus but used the more colorful Anglo-Saxon terms that all teenagers knew. We argued for some time with most of the boys siding with me. I was persuasive. Eventually even the more educated boy began to waver. Maybe his parents didn't really know all they thought they did. When the argument ended with a closing and very poignant point that I made the other boy conceded that I was right all along. I said, "Use your head. Which is bigger?" I left more ignorant than I started but triumphant nonetheless. I can only hope that the other kid finally learned the truth and wasn't consigned to having to believe the misinformation I had convinced him with was the truth.

One day my sister complained that the man who lived across the street from us was "playing with himself" as he watched the little girls in the neighborhood. My Dad questioned her at length. The man in question was known in the neighborhood as "weird". He used to play a harmonica on the steps in front of his house and would serenade the neighborhood in a loud voice.

Dad called the police and tried to lodge a complaint against the man. The police questioned Dad at length and finally determined that the man had been inside his home and had pulled the curtains aside as he masturbated while watching the little neighborhood girls. The police said they could do nothing as the man was inside his home. Dad then told them to "forget the complaint" and that he would personally take care of the problem. The startled police told him to wait and they would visit him and talk about it.

The result was that the man was placed under arrest and had to appear in court after spending a night in jail. My Dad attended the court session and told me about it later. He said that the prosecuting attorney questioned the man saying, "Mr. Smith, do you masturbate"? The man quickly replied that he didn't. The prosecutor then said, "Do you know what masturbation is"? The man shook his head "no". The prosecutor then shouted, "Have you ever jacked off"?

The now thoroughly cowed man tearfully replied, "Yes, yes, but I'll never do it again". After the laughter in the room subsided the judge lectured the man concerning his conduct and told him of the apprehension among his neighbors who were only trying to protect their daughters. The man was given probation. The problem went away and was not repeated.

Dad tried to support any and all religious activities that were happening in the area. I was required to attend any Baptist church "camps" that were formed during the summertime. I was ambivalent concerning the whole idea but since it was suggested and I had no other things to occupy my time I went willingly along with the idea. That is not to say that I bought into the whole concept by any means. I had my own ideas about churches and religion in general. I refused to be pushed into something that I didn't believe in just to placate some pontificating adult.

Dad and I always had arguments about religion. I believed that a God existed and that there was a system of morals that needed to be adhered to in order to please God and to facilitate an orderly and moral society. Other than that, things were up to discussion. Dad never brooked any discussions concerning religion. Things were as they were, end of argument. If I asked a question about the Bible it meant that I was a borderline heathen. If I persisted then it was written that I was not only a heathen but also an unbeliever, an agnostic, even an atheist. I learned at an early age not to question, at least not to offer a question to Dad. Plenty of questions popped up in my head but I knew better than to ask them of Dad. I relied on my intuitive intelligence and read as much as I could. I could hardly ask any questions of any preachers or pastors I knew as they were sure to tell my father about my failings in my belief.

Attitudes such as these did not disappear when I went to church or bible camp. I went along with all of the de rigueur things that were required of all campers. We were not to smoke, dance, date, fornicate, wear suggestive clothing, kiss anyone of the other sex, kiss anyone of the same sex, speak of sex, think of sex, exhibit an awareness that something called sex even existed or give an appearance of "worldliness" whatever the hell that was all about. Everyone seemed to have a girlfriend in the camp and I was no exception. You weren't supposed to "do" anything with your girlfriend but that didn't stop some sinners. I "did" everything I could think of with my girlfriend but as I was young and uninitiated I didn't exactly "sin" as far as the Baptists were concerned.

Since my father was a Baptist Preacher I was expected to attend any and all functions that the church deemed correct for a young person to participate in. Dad was connected to a church in Saginaw, Michigan at this time and we used to spend all day on Sundays in Saginaw going to church and having a social time with several of the congregation. Sundays were by and large pleasant and I made several friends but I was still considered an outsider as we were not from the farming community and did not live in the area. Still, I made friends with one of the Polish girls who abounded there. She was pretty (as far as I was concerned) but just a trifle "basic" even at that precocious stage in my life. If I had been accused of being an elitist at that time I guess I would have to have concurred with that assessment. The odd thing about that was that I was far from being considered anything approaching an elite person. I came from humble antecedents and my family could be considered as "poor" by any of several yardsticks. Nevertheless, I was a voracious reader and read any and everything I could get my hands on. I had some well-developed attitudes and values even at this early age and so a well-meaning farm girl from the middle of Michigan fell a little short of the mark but she was quite acceptable for the time being. Besides, it wasn't likely that the relationship would ever progress to a carnal ending. I was, after all, the "preacher's kid" and, as such, was expected to conduct myself accordingly. I was well aware that I was being "watched" by any number of people who were just waiting for the opportunity to satisfy their prurient dreams by throwing rocks at me for any slight transgression. My Father reminded me of this as often as I could be persuaded to listen. So it was that I contented myself with holding hands and stealing a kiss every chance I had.

It was summertime and the church offered the young folk an opportunity to attend a church camp. It was de rigueur that I attend, of course. I don't remember being given a choice. One day I was informed that I was going and that was that. The camp was in the northern part of Michigan and it was beautiful there. The food was adequate and there was plenty of free time. The price one had to pay for this communing with nature was to attend church services three times a day. I privately thought that was a little much but no one had ever asked my opinion about anything at all least religious matters so I went along just like I went along with just about everything in life. I consider that I was a student of people in general even then. Accordingly I thought it strange that the student body, universally against carnal knowledge sans marriage, would pair off at every opportunity and wander into the woods to commune with nature in their own ways. I didn't know the meaning of the word, hypocrite, at the time but I knew the symptoms. I got along by going along. I ate three meals per day, attended any outings that were offered and attended church ad nauseum. There were precious few books to read other than the bible and I had read that long ago. I was bored.

One day the church found a missionary who wished to preach to the residents of the camp. He was welcomed with open arms. He held services as often as he could, fervently preaching, sweating, throwing his arms around and generally burning up calories at a rapid rate. He was very persuasive. One evening he gave an alter call. For those of you who are unfamiliar with an alter call it is an opportunity for anyone in the general congregation to come forward if they feel called by the Almighty to some specific purpose. A good purpose in this instance would be a call or feeling that God wanted you to become a missionary in some far away place. As the missionary sweated, preached and implored the young folk to give their lives to God a special feeling came over the congregation. Young minds were caught up in the fervency of the moment. Young people have emotions that are very close to the surface and are easily ignited, especially by expert mind manipulators like missionary preachers. Kids started to cry as emotions spilled over and they began to file toward the alter. I watched with awe as the missionary worked the emotions of the crowd. Every one was mesmerized. Everyone but me. One by one the kids streamed to the alter, tears running down their cheeks. Everyone, it seemed, felt that they had been called by God to become a missionary to some far off place. As I watched the thought struck me that the more educated of the converts, that is, the ones who had a more general knowledge of geography, were very well received by the missionary, who would crow about the place the convert had been called to. Such far off places like Afghanistan, Liberia, Somaliland and New Guinea were met with noises of awe. Imagine the Lord calling someone to places like that! I stood where I was as everyone in the whole congregation trotted down to the alter. I was simply amazed. I couldn't believe what was happening. I believe to this day that I witnessed a mass hypnosis. Why I wasn't affected I don't know. Perhaps it was because I had an inquiring mind or because I was used to thinking for myself. Who really knows? What transpired, finally, was that the whole church congregation except for myself was present at the alter. Everyone was looking at me. The missionary was continuing the alter call. Obviously he would not be content until everyone was at the alter professing a call to some far away country. He was looking for one hundred percent. The music continued and the missionary continued to hoarsely call for converts. I finally turned and left the church. I was disgusted. I knew a play on emotions even if I couldn't adequately define it at that time. It was a cheap shot as far as I was concerned. It took several days before the rest of the kids would associate with "the sinner", also known as me.

The camp councilors took the kids to one of the Great Lakes every day or so in order to swim. It was nice as the bus ride was usually fairly long and the scenery in northern Michigan was very pretty. The actual swim period was a drag as the male swimmers had to wear long tee shirts in order to cover up the repugnant male bodies occasioned by the wearing of normal swim trunks. Or perhaps the councilors were afraid that the female bathers would go wild at the sight of the hairless chests and attempt a battery on the males in a hysteric sexual orgy. Who knows? At any rate I hated swimming with a floppy tee shirt encumbering my body. Then one day God intervened. The local office of the Coast Guard decided to look us over and decided that the wearing of loose floppy shirts was a danger to the swimmer and so the shirts were discarded to the distinct relief of the males. The camp lasted for about two weeks. I was ecstatic when it was over and I could go home to my books.

Back home railroad trains were out as far as excitement went so we needed something else to pass the time. Every boy had a BB gun back then so we decided to have BB gun wars. We were aware of the dangers BBs presented to our eyes so we made a rule that no one could fire at any combatant as long as the only target seen was the enemy's head. The battlefield would be a storage yard containing acres of structural steel just made for climbing around on and firing at will. A BB could not hurt the steel. We figured that we couldn't be hurt either. Remember the old adage that says, "No good military plan survives the first shot fired"? In the fog of war anything can happen.

We were in a pitched battle. I had personally accounted for two dead enemy combatants when one of the Hun fired at my face as I peered around a pile of structural steel. The BB hit me between the centerline of my nose and my right eye. The war was called off as all of the combatants gathered around me and tried to assess the damage. Other than the way it hurt the only evidence of the wound was a perfect circle where the BB had bruised my face. My eye was untouched. You could hardly tell that I had been shot by a BB; unless you were blind, that is. I knew that my father would not allow the war wound to go unnoticed.

The warring factions called a temporary truce and retired to our respective homes. I hid the BB gun so that the possibility of associating it with the neon sign on my face would be reduced.

When my Dad came home I made sure that he only saw the left side of my face. I couldn't keep up the ruse forever and eventually he caught sight of the reddish-blue circle near my eye.

"What's that round spot near your eye?"

"Oh, I just stumbled into something. You know how clumsy I am."

Indeed he did. The self-denigrating criticism confirmed my Dad's suspicions concerning me so he let the subject drop much to my relief. If he had pursued his line of questioning he surely would have confiscated my BB gun and perhaps would have appended a wound to my posterior as well. The Jesuit adage that the ends justify the means was a lifesaver.

We were much more careful when the next war rolled around.

I always hated the common sports of football, baseball, basketball and tidily-winks. I tended to gravitate toward camping, hiking, hunting, marksmanship and orienteering, (although that term hadn't been invented yet.) My friend Tom and I had joined the Boy Scouts and were associated with a troop that was sponsored by the Salvation Army. Prior to this time I had given the Salvation Army little thought other than to make fun of the "Starvation Army". I quickly discovered that the organization was a wonderful one and was only concerned with doing good for downtrodden people and incidentally telling them about the word of God in the bargain. The Army went out of its way to make a Boy Scout troop a first rate one for the boys involved. I've always had a soft spot for the organization following my association with them. Dad had reservations concerning the Salvationists but then he differed with any type of faith other than the Southern Baptist click grouping all other faiths in the term "isms". I was more of a live and let live person and as long as any faith believed in God and his Son I could put up with just about any other "odd" ideas. Dad differed, of course, but as long as I didn't exactly attend church services at any Salvation Army churches he condoned my association.

Tom and I swiftly graduated from the Boy Scouts to the Explorer Scouts because of our age. The Scout leader was an aging man named Leonard Hodges. He was completely unselfish of his time as concerned the Boy Scouts and had been involved with them for many years. Tom and I formed a sort of tripartite group with Mr. Hodges as we were of an age that allowed us to lead the younger scouts. We did so in troop campouts, jamborees and weekly camping trips. I became adept in the art of living out of doors and being comfortable while doing so. I was willing to teach anyone who wanted to learn those skills how to do so and, in so doing, passed many happy days and nights. My life was full; I was happy. I became adept at tracking and was privileged, one day, to witness a little weasel I had tracked dip his paw into a pool of water and flee in an attempt to make me think that he had entered the water. Little glimpses like that into the real nature of things was very important to me and I think that I became a better person for them. I learned to value life and so I laid hunting aside. Not completely, mind you, but I could not countenance, any longer, the senseless killing of nature's beautiful creatures without cause. I learned to value the thought processes of wild creatures as they tried to survive in a sometimes-harsh world. My biology teachers would castigate me accusing me of the cardinal sin of anthropomorphism but I treated those teachers like I treated my father. I had my own ideas as to how things worked and, since their theories and hypotheses could not be empirically proven I figured that mine were just as good.

I learned how to make a fire without matches, how to bed down without a bed or blankets, how to forage and eat without food as we usually know it, how to stay warm in cold weather without wool clothing, how to stay cool in hot weather without air conditioning, how to evade and how to track. I learned survival traits before I even knew those things were taught in the military units that I eventually came to be part of.

Mr. Hodges told me that the Salvation Army had agreed to sponsor a scout to go to the giant jamboree at Valley Forge, Pennsylvania that summer. He told me that I was the choice of the sponsors if I wanted to go. It was a wonderful opportunity and I leapt at it. My parents gave their OK and soon I was part of a large contingent of scouts and scoutmasters driving to Valley Forge. It was a wonderful journey for a young boy whose parents could never have afforded the trip let alone the jamboree. The Buick Motor Division of General Motors loaned the group about 50 new Buicks for the trip. We slept at several colleges and universities along the way that volunteered the space and time for the event. At Valley Forge we slept in tents and teepees, cooking our own food, cleaning up our own messes and associating with Boy Scouts from all over the world. I wondered at a group of Scouts from Lithuania who had a memorial to scouts who had been killed by the Communists. I had never heard of an animal called a Communist and asked questions about them. My education was beginning. I remember large campfires with thousands of Scouts in attendance. It was a wonderful time and a wonderful event.

One day my Scoutmaster approached me and said, "Would you like to be a member of the Siamese Royal Order of Campers?" Of course I would. I was open to anything and everything that had to do with scouting activities. Later on that night I was led to a campfire that was surrounded by about a thousand Scouts. A full dozen of us were supposed to be made members of "the order" that evening. I don't think any of us ever asked just why we had been singled out for this singular honor. It was enough that we had been so singularly picked. At the appropriate time we all lined up beside the fire. Soon a large man dressed in a robe and a turban strode purposefully out and stood in front of us. He made a long speech about how he had been a friend of the King of Siam and how he had saved the King's life. He said the King had commissioned him to find and draft other stalwart, intelligent, strong and handsome converts to the Order the king had formed in honor of the turbaned man. After his speech he wheeled around and addressed us.

"You supplicants! Do you promise on your honor to uphold the wonderful tenants of the Royal Order of Siam?" We stood there like dummies not knowing what to do. "Speak!" the turbaned man roared. "Say 'Yes, I promise,'" he roared. We all screamed, "Yes, I promise."

"You must do one more thing to be a member of the Royal Order," he screamed. "You must kiss the royal ring, given to me by the King of Siam." He thrust out his arm. A large ring was apparent on his hand. "Kiss the ring!" he screamed.

We all were kneeling in front of him as ordered earlier. As he passed before us we all tried to kiss the ring. As we did he intoned, "You must chant the oath. Say after me." We all parroted.

"Ohhh." We all intoned, "ohhhh."

"Ohhwatta." We parroted, "ohwatta."

"Ohwattagoo." We hummed, "ohwattagoo."

"OhwatagooSiam," he shouted. "Oh watta goo Siam," we shouted.

"Louder and faster," he screamed.

"OHWATTAGOOSIAM," we screamed.

"Again." He was getting louder and more insistent. We continued to scream, "Oh Whatta Goose I Am!"

"You're telling me," he announced and turning on his heel he disappeared. The assembly was rolling on the ground laughing. Slowly we all realized what had happened. I shook my head and laughed at my own embarrassment. I always knew that I was gullible. This proved it. It was all good fun and nobody was harmed.

My troop was known as "The Wolves". We drank water from Lister bags laced with chlorine tablets and cooked our meals over wood fires. Cooks were selected by a watch bill made up by the Scout Leaders. We always said a prayer before eating. Scouts believed in God and that belief was enunciated in the Scout pledge. Years later the Boy Scout program would weather many assaults on its beliefs and its creed but this was 1950 and things were different then. Heroes were clear-cut, as were enemies. The Scout program has always been and always will be a wonderful program for young people. Scouting personifies the value system that started our country. Today it has its distracters and those who would tear that wonderful organization to pieces but so far it has had some very staunch heroes who persist in keeping to the old ways. It is my perennial prayer that they may remain steadfast in that regard. Bad cess to those who rail at the organization.

A troop of Scouts camping next door to the Wolves were a group of older boys from the upper peninsula of Michigan. They were well schooled in camping, skiing, ski jumping, hunting and other outdoor skills. I admired them immensely. They seemed to know so much. One of them talked at great length to me about knives in general, a subject that I had always loved. The other Scout believed that steel made in Great Britain was superior to anything made. Sheffield steel, according to him, was the epitome of steel. I had never thought about steel at all. A knife was a knife as far as I was concerned. These discussions were the basis for my life-long search for edged weapons in general and whetted my thirst for any and all knowledge about edged weapons. I remembered all of those discussions later on in life when I took up fencing with the foil, the saber and the epee.

I was a dry sponge in those days, an empty vessel. I soaked up knowledge in any form, especially that body of knowledge that dealt with the out-of-doors, with living close to nature, with animals and with firearms, marksmanship and survival, although it wasn't called survival then. It was considered a skill such as the frontiersmen possessed and I excelled in it.

I remained in the Scout Troop when I returned home and when my age permitted it I became an Explorer Scout and a Troop Camp leader. I led younger scouts in the mysteries of pitching tents, cooking outdoors on wood fires, building fires from scratch, weathering foul weather in camp and building things like bridges and towers from logs and rope bindings. Scouting was a great way for a young boy to keep out of trouble but it wasn't foolproof.

I had gotten interested in Indian lore in the scouting program. I had learned some of the Plains Indian sign language and soaked up any information available about the way our indigenous people lived. I was fascinated about how they could stalk prey and tried hard to emulate them. I had made friends with several Chippewa Indians while I lived in St. Charles. I became adept at quiet movement through the woods and stalking other Scouts along with the indigenous animals in the area through scouting games and exercises. I was proud of my accomplishments and fancied that I was as good as or better than any Indian trying to snare his dinner. Tom and I attended any scout get-togethers we could, competing in exercises designed to show off the skills the scouts practiced. We always came away with honors.

The Salvation Army encouraged the competition and made it possible for us to attend as many competitions as possible. There will always be a soft spot in my heart for the Salvation Army for their efforts in making it possible for a few kids with no resources to participate in all of those events.

Kids will persist on being kids. Competition is rife and no one wishes to be the "goat" when it comes to "who is best". Both Tom and I heard of a school for well-off girls in the country that was having a few problems with some kids our age. It seemed that the school or summer camp was housed in an old mansion in the country surrounded by two six-foot iron fences and lots of trees and shrubs. It was a beautiful and isolated place. The problem was that kids had figured out that it would be lots of fun to climb the daunting fences and harass the girls. Why would kids want to climb high iron fences, subject themselves to hardship and the very distinct possibility of being arrested and incarcerated just to scare and alarm a few girls? I guess the answer is the old one of "because they are there", the excitement of the chase and the obvious challenge. Teenagers have always thought that they are immortal. The caretakers of the place would have to chase the harassers and the evasion of the chasers was heady and exciting play. The kids attended the same school as Tom and I did and bragged that the guards on the school property had never captured them. Both Tom and I sneered at the braggarts and an argument ensued over just how hard it was to evade an old guard. Challenges were laid down and accepted and soon Tom and I found ourselves in the place of having to come up with a better system of bearding the goat in order to prove our expertise in field craft.

We got our heads together and came up with a plan to harass the girls in their secure environment, to cause as much harmless distress as possible and to, of course, get away scot-free. We posed the plan to our detractors and were scoffed at. Thus armed with resolve we decided to go ahead with our plan.

We had reconnoitered the place before we put our plan in action. We knew that the girls, who were of our age, were housed on the top floor of a three-story mansion. An iron fire escape to the third floor would allow the girls to escape in case of a fire but it also allowed access to their sleeping quarters. We had examined the place at length one evening without being detected. This gave us added confidence in our abilities to accumulate intelligence and evade.

On the night the mission was to be activated I went to bed at a normal time. Then, when my parents had gone to bed, I arose, dressed in "Indian" garb, which included a breech clout and leggings, face paint and feathers in my hair, and exited the house via the second story window, over the roof and down a rain spout. We were determined that we would dress and act like Indians. Tom had already left his house and we met at a pre-arranged spot. We painted our faces and, as we did, I thought of my ancestors who painted themselves with blue woad and fought their battles without clothing. We trotted toward the target, several miles distant. We had to cross a wide stream to get to our destination and we did so via a railroad trestle. The stream widened out at that spot to a large fen or swamp. We walked across the trestle and soon were up against the iron fence.

The fence consisted of six-foot uprights that were topped with arrow-type points to discourage climbing. Tom and I had cut our teeth on fences of this type. We had excelled in getting over fences that were ten feet in height and were made of wood. We also had learned how to overcome iron fences of this type. This was just another exercise and was fun as far as we were concerned. I made a stirrup of my hands and Tom ran onto the fence, stuck his foot in the stirrup and was vaulted over to the top of the fence. He was the heaviest of us and needed the help. I then backed up and, running at the fence, hit it with one foot and jumped upward. Tom, who had stayed atop the fence, reached down and caught my up thrown arm, hauling me on top of the palisade. The whole exercise had occupied all of about 20 seconds. It was easy.

Once over the outer fence we repeated the exercise for the inner fence and were home. We knelt inside the fence, panting, and listened for any enemy. All was quiet. We were undetected. We grinned at each other through our face paint and quietly crept toward the mansion proper. The first surprise was when we encountered a wall tent pitched on the grounds on the way to the building. The tent was occupied and was lighted by candle lanterns. A radio offered solace to the inhabitant.

We walked around the tent without being detected by the inhabitant, whoever he was. We found that there was only one person in the tent and surmised that he was probably a guard of some sort. We discounted him as ineffectual and carried on with the task we had set for ourselves.

We approached the manor house and located the iron fire escape that extended all the way to the roof. Tom made a stirrup with his hands this time and I used the aid to leap up and grab the lower portion of the iron ladder, pulling it down so that we could use it to climb to the third story. We made the climb silently and were soon crouched on the third story balcony. It was a little later than midnight and everything was silent. The girls were all asleep. We could see inside the dormitory and the rows of beds were readily apparent. The girls were snoring in secure bliss.

Tom had brought along a large hairy paw that we had purchased somewhere in a flight of fancy. It seemed to be a correct thing to have at the time. The windows on the third story were open as it was summer and there were no screens on them. Tom put the paw onto his hand and approached the nearest window. He grunted and growled just like a bear would. Tom and I had studied the vocal emanations of the indigenous animals in our area and knew what a bear sounded like. The girl in the bed nearest the window tossed and suddenly froze as she awoke and listened to the bear. Tom reached over and covered her face with the paw. He growled as he did so. The effect was as desired; the girl screamed and ran from the bear spreading panic as she did. Lights came on all of a sudden and activity emanated as if the sun had suddenly come up. Alarms rang. People ran amok, bouncing off of walls and screaming. The result was entirely satisfactory.

Tom and I ran down the fire escape laughing as we did so. In fact we were laughing so hard that it was hard to get down the iron escape. We hit the bottom of the escape and ran toward the tent where the "guard" was housed. Without comment or plan we separated at the tent and each of us ran around a separate side. As we ran we pulled up the tent stakes. The tent collapsed to the tune of curses of the inhabitant. We ignored him as we ran toward the fence. We repeated the drill of getting over the fence once again and did it again at the second fence.

We ran toward the fen congratulating ourselves that we had successfully completed the mission. We were laughing and cracking jokes. Tomorrow we would brag to our contemporaries about how we had "counted coup" on the "enemy", just as the plains Indians had done years ago. Suddenly there was a loud "crack" or "bang" and something whizzed through the trees near us. Someone was firing at us, shooting at us with a handgun. Fear gave speed to our flight.

"Jesus Christ," Tom yelled as we sped onward.

"They're shooting at us," I yelled as I tried to keep up with him.

We conserved our breath as we sped along. We entered the fen or swamp and kept relatively dry by hopping from hassock to hassock, stepping on the little sprouts of swamp grass in an effort to keep out of the sucking mud. Apparently the guard had lost track of us or simply didn't wish to enter the swampy area as no more shots were fired in our direction. We slowed down and oriented ourselves in an attempt to find out how we could get home. The night was clear and the stars were out. We didn't have a compass and didn't need one. We knew the area and knew how to get home.

We made our way toward the railway trestle, as it was the easiest way to cross the stream and get home. As we approached the trestle we saw, to our distress, that a police officer had parked his car so as to shine its lights onto the trestle in order to illuminate anyone crossing the bridge. We had studied what the Boy Scouts taught to the military in Great Britain during World War II and knew that they had taught that the correct way to cross a railway trestle was to get between the rails and hunker along, staying between the rails. The English scouts emphasized that the large "Smoky Bear" wide brimmed hat should be worn so as to reduce its profile. We didn't have hats like that but the teaching was otherwise appropriate. We stretched out along the rail keeping our heads down so that our white faces would not be illuminated and seen. Then we slid over the rail and humped along the ties. The bright light illuminated the sky above us but we were safe in the shadow between the rails. We humped along and finally arrived at the end of the trestle undiscovered. We were filthy and disheveled but happy in the knowledge that we had escaped and evaded.

We crept home and managed to go to bed without our parent's knowledge. We slept soundly knowing that we were better than those hunting us but we never attempted to repeat the stunt again.

The stunt was not my finest hour but it was done in fun and the competitive spirit of "bearding the goat". In retrospect it was "bullying", something of which I have always held in abject contempt. I am shamed when I think about it.

The Scout program was one of the best things a boy could hope for. I worked on merit badges and worked hard on the entire program. It was a superb program and one that will always make America's young religious, honest, reliable and dependable. It is one of the best programs for young people that could ever be envisioned. The time I spent in the Scouting program was arguably some of the best time I ever had during my formative years.

My family wasn't exactly poor but we weren't well off either. We always had to watch the pennies and I think that made us closer and wiser than most. I used to carry my lunch in a brown paper sack. After I had eaten the lunch the sack had to be smoothed out, folded and placed in my right hip pocket to be carried home and reused the next day. I was allowed only one sack per week. If I transgressed and allowed the sack to be torn then I had to carry the lunch any way I thought appropriate since I was not given another one. I always felt the lack of funds especially when other, more fortunate kids, tended to flaunt their family's wealth.

One episode stays with me over the years. It was prom time. That's prom as in a Junior High School prom; not as important as a real high school prom but important nevertheless. I had a girl friend that I wished to invite but was reticent because I really didn't have any clothes appropriate for a prom. I agonized over the whole thing and had tendered the invitation, which was accepted immediately much to my delight. I knew that I would have to cough up money enough for a large corsage, which was de rigueur for a prom at that time. The damned corsages always got in the way of everything any one wanted to do and were too expensive. The really expensive ones also made the girl's dress droop due to the weight of the flowers. They were necessary though, just like the little melons the Japanese buy for exorbitant amounts of Yen to give as gifts. Everybody knows that the damned things are too expensive but buying them shows the flag and the idea that the recipient of the gift is worth every penny. Mom knew all about that and suggested that perhaps my girlfriend would like a single flower to wear on her dress. It would not cost much and would be much more comfortable. Beautiful idea! I broached the subject to the girlfriend and held my breath for the answer. When it came I was deflated. I had discounted the status symbol the corsages afforded the girls. Bigger was better. She wanted a corsage.

I had made up my mind that an old hand-me-down suit I had obtained from a friend of the family would probably do but conversations with some of my friends disabused me of that idea. The pack leader excitedly propounded the idea that "we should all wear our maroon trousers and white jackets". The other fellow travelers all clamored that the idea was a bully one. I was stunned. What ever gave this fellow the idea that I had any access to something like a white jacket and maroon trousers? That was like asking me to drive a Lincoln Continental to the prom. I couldn't believe that anyone would be such an elitist as to presume that every young boy would possess items like those suggested. The thought stuck in my throat and still does to this day. At the time I didn't know what elitism was but I sure knew what its effects were. They made you feel bad, poor and ineffectual. I made some sort of neutral response and cleared the area.

I attended the prom with my girlfriend and her huge corsage, which gave her status of some sort, and avoided the other guys who showed up in their white jackets and maroon trousers, congratulating themselves and preening for the worshiping female empty heads. I was happy to be on the outside as always. Never the joiner, I had fun in my own way and I know my girlfriend did also. Bad cess to the mob and the joiners. Independence ran in my family and I was probably the epitome of the independent, anarchistic teenager anywhere around.

The Junior High School I attended was situated in a fallow area wherein several shallow ponds were located. In the spring of the year hundreds of tiny spring frogs would suddenly sprout up around the area. They were a wonderful harbinger of spring and were welcome as far as I was concerned but were an anathema as far as the females in the immediate area were concerned. One day during a lunch break an idea occurred to me. Why not scoop up a number of these tiny denizens of the swamp and introduce them to my mathematics teacher? She was a nice person but seemed to need some spicing up in my opinion.

Normally I was required to save my lunch sack, folding it carefully each day in order to place it in my right back pocket in order to give it back to my Mother for a refill the next day. I was a creature of habit. My billfold went into my left hip pocket and everything else went into the right. That habit remains to this day. Paper sacks cost money and we had little to spare. One paper sack was supposed to last me a whole week. In the present instance, however, the precious sack seemed to be much more utilitarian if used as a receptacle for about a hundred little frogs. The more I thought about it the better the idea seemed. I scooped up about sixty or so of the little creatures and placed them carefully in the paper sack. I placed the sack under my desk when I attended the math class intending to let them loose when the class was dismissed.

I didn't count on the moisture the little frogs brought with them. The sack became wet and lost its integrity as the frogs escaped and began to hop about the classroom. The first indication anyone had that anything was amiss was when the nervous teacher remarked, "Oh! My! There's a frog!" She picked up a sheet of paper and used it to pick up the frog, which she threw out of a window. Immediately after that she said, "Oh! My! There's another one. Look, another one. Ohhhh." Frogs were suddenly abundant in the classroom.

A little fink who was seated next to me suddenly ran to the front of the classroom and whispered into the teacher's ear. It didn't take much imagination to figure out what he was telling her as both of them were looking at me. The teacher, putting on her most severe look, called out, "Edward, will you please come up here?"

Edward. No one ever called me that unless I was in trouble. Oh, well, I'd been there before. I presented myself to the math teacher.

"Edward, do you know anything about all of these frogs?"

"Yes'um, they're all mine."

"All right, Edward, you may stay after the bell rings and catch all of them. Then you may come here after school lets out and stay for an hour or two to clean up the classroom."

"Yes'um". Fair was fair. I was caught and would have to pay the penance but so would the little fink who had squealed on me. I told him what was in store for him and later on I administered what is normally known as corporal punishment on his body. It was only right.

A little aside is in order here. Many years later I was married and had purchased a home in Naples, Florida. My wife had found a person who had agreed to put up some draperies for her. She was bubbly about him, telling me that he had attended the same junior high school we both had attended. I was noncommittal about a drapery person but soon he appeared. As soon as he saw me his face hardened and he gave every attribute of being hostile. It was the same little fink that had told the math teacher that I was the culprit who had unleashed the horrible little frogs. As soon as I saw him and the look on his face I instantaneously knew what was going on. He still harbored a grudge all of these years about his thumping for the sin of finking on a classmate. I immediately burst out laughing. My wife didn't know what was so funny and I couldn't tell her until the little fink had left. We never saw him again. By the way, his draperies were poorly installed and did not survive six months. I thought that it was only fitting that a little fink would become an installer of inferior draperies.

It was about this time that I began to have medical problems. I felt sick a lot and my stomach seemed queasy. I complained to my parents and they took me to a doctor who said that I had a hernia that had to be "taken care of". I was placed in a hospital and an operation was performed to "reduce a hydrocele". While I was there the doctors found that what was really making me feel ill was an enlarged appendix that was about to burst. The appendix was removed at the same time. I left the hospital feeling weak and ineffectual. I was told that I could not engage in any sports for a year.

The sports thing didn't bother me at all. I never had any inclination to play any of the regular sports anyway. I liked camping, fishing, shooting and outdoor sports like that. I hated baseball, football and basketball. The so-called "organized sports" were not at all in my library of things that were admired, liked or even tolerated. I was a maverick and was happy being one.

Junior High School is probably akin to a small town when it comes to everyone knowing everything about everyone. It wasn't a week before every kid in the whole school knew that I had undergone an operation and that I was supposed to "take it easy" for a year afterwards. My life was an open book.

Soon after that I had an altercation with a much larger student named Merle. He was a "moose" in colloquial terms and was secure in the knowledge that he could hammer me into submission in record time. I, of course, was intractable, and made it known that I would meet the moose on the field of battle with the intent of tearing off his head and shoving it up his backside. Everyone knew that my braggadocio was just that and that I wasn't capable of doing anything at all like what I said I would do. Everyone showed up all the same in order to see someone get hammered. It didn't really matter who got hammered just so someone did. The blood lust was up and the populi were ready to see the lions eat the Christians.

At the appointed time and place the school turned out en masse in order to see a little blood. The event might as well have been printed in the school paper. The only no-shows were the teachers who, as always, were ignorant of what goes on in a junior high school. I made my way through the cheering crowd to the sound of well-wishers who goaded me on to a bloody victory. No one cheered for my opponent as he was held in general contempt by most of the students who avoided him simply because he was a large, dangerous bully. I was singular in my stupidity in bracing such an opponent.

As I entered the extemporaneous arena made by the crowd who had formed a circle in our honor I saw my opponent who was being shoved about by several of the larger students who were attempting to entice him into the center of the field of combat by thrusting him farther into the circle with admonitions of "Get out there, you fucking chicken". Needless to say this did not calm my opponent in the least and I wished that the cheering section would not ruffle his feathers so much. I had already steeled myself for a beating but thought that it was better to be beaten than to give in to a bully. Better to accept one beating than to live a dog's life of cowering because a bully thought that he owned you. I only wished for a benevolent whipping and not one that was prompted by the maddening crowd urging my worthy opponent to greater excesses by virtue of making fun of him. In addition I had the unrealistic thought that I might just be allowed a few blows that would bring real pain to my opponent. My only thought at this time was to account for myself in such a way as to not bring shame on myself.

My opponent met me at the center of the arena. "You fucker," he offered, "I'm going to whip your ass unless you apologize."

In all honesty I couldn't remember just what I was supposed to apologize for. It made absolutely no difference. I wouldn't have apologized at that moment for being born let alone for some nebulous slight on the person of this oaf. In all truth, anything I could have said against his person that would have alienated him would have been a compliment as far as I was concerned. He was, in my estimation, a low-life, un-educated, abrasive, overbearing, pushy bully who gloried in strong-arming other kids who either couldn't or wouldn't defend them selves. I was not about to be counted in that number.

I squared away with him, fists up and ready and offered the ultimate insult that was guaranteed to start the fracas. "Your mother wears combat boots. Fuck your whole family including your ugly sister." Merle responded with a roundhouse right that connected with my head and left me with my ears ringing and my vision blurred. I countered with two ineffectual swings that absolutely decimated the air and nothing else as Merle artfully dodged and cocked his huge fist in an attempt to administer the coup-de-grace as quickly as possible before any of the teachers saw the massed gathering and came out to break up the fight. Suddenly I was jerked backwards so forcefully that I sprawled on the ground. A very large black student named James Brown had decided to come to my aid figuring correctly that I was entirely out of my league.

James was only an acquaintance of mine. I knew who and what he was but we didn't exactly circulate in the same circles. James came from, you might say, the other side of the tracks. James did have a well-proportioned sense of fair play, perhaps because he had fought in the Golden Gloves contests for a couple of years in a row. His trainer had instilled a good sense of fairness and sportsmanship in his charge. James had not only fought but had won every match he had participated in. He was, what you might say, a very worthy opponent. He was bulky, fast and self confident and garnered respect wherever he went. As he threw me backwards he growled, "You stay the fuck out of the way". One didn't argue with James.

James faced Merle and spat, "You scared to fight?"

At this point Merle had several options but he unwisely chose the least most acceptable. He stuck out his chin and said, "I ain't afraid to fight anyone".

James Brown hit Merle Carson squarely on the chin with enough force to sail his head into the next county. Merle's eyes immediately caged and he collapsed into a heap with his legs involuntarily threshing spasmodically in the "fight or flight" response as he was "out" without a count. There was no doubt in anyone's mind which involuntary choice Merle's body was trying to accomplish. The "fight" had lasted less than one minute. James walked away without any comment. The crowd broke up recounting every blow and embellishing each one. The next day you wouldn't recognize the fight from the accounts being bandied about already. James was a hero. Merle was a goat and I didn't even figure in the telling. I never did figure out just why James came to my aid but I suspect that he was exuberant in his confidence about his abilities and simply wanted to prove them. He never talked to me about the incident but I heard that he had told friends that he was not going to allow me to get hurt, as he had heard about my hospitalization and operations. I didn't know what to make of the report but assumed that James just loved to fight. In any case, I owed him, big time.

I picked myself up, wiped the blood off my nose and headed for home. My parents were used to, by this time, me coming home bloody and beaten, made no comment. They figured that if I needed help I would ask for it. Merle avoided me assiduously after the incident.

It was about this time my folks moved from Thrift City to the north of the city of Flint. It was a step up socially as far as society was concerned but I had always thought that the tiny house in Thrift City was comfortable and suited me. With the new move I was forced to commute to school and took a city bus into town where I had to transfer to another bus that would take me to school. Along the way I noticed two other kids who took the second bus each day. They were a sister and younger brother and appeared to be rather poor and shabby. I felt sorry for them for some reason. The sister always looked out for the little brother and my heart went out to them although we never communicated in any manner. Much later on I would find out that they attended a Lutheran school in the area. They remained in my mind for some reason and would resurrect as friends later.

In my new home I had my own room, a luxury I never had prior to this. My father was preaching, by this time, in a small church in an area north of Flint but close to our new home. It was a comfortable arrangement. It was also pretty lonely in that my old friends in Thrift City were far away. I kept in touch with them via the conduit of the scouting program; another good thing that came out of that fine program.

I attended the junior high "sock hops" and the "graduation ball" with my longtime girl friend Betty Cantrell. I had already formed lasting alliances in accord with my deep convictions that encompassed loyalty and obligation. My girl friend was probably the first example of this attitude as I stayed close to her for years, even at this early age. Much, much later on I learned of the Japanese duty to Giri and On, two words that do not even begin to describe the national loyalty to obligation. In the Western world we think of the word "obligation" as something that we should do. If we don't then there are social sanctions. To the Japanese mind obligation is something that you must live with all of your life. There's obligation to self, parents, siblings, family, friends, country and religion. Obligation is omnipresent and you pay homage to the obligation any way you can. Failure to do so is unthinkable. It causes you to lose "face" or respect, something that can cause one to commit seppuku or the taking of one's life by ceremonial means. Seppuku is the ultimate apology by apologizing with one's life. In the Western world we do not think of obligation in so rigid a way but we do have very definite ideas of the concept. One example of this is the notion of "going steady". For a young person in junior high school "going steady" is a real commitment and is probably as serious a matter to that person as Giri is to a Japanese.

I "went steady" with Betty off and on for years until we finally parted company in what I considered was a tumultuous and soul-wrenching episode. I'd like to think that Betty felt the same but I have my doubts. It was all part of "growing up".

I can honestly say that my liaisons with the opposite sex were always instigated by the girls in question. I was always shy and withdrawn when it came to girls. They were intimidating. I guess that I was always afraid of the possibility of rejection, something that was far more serious to a teenager than to an adult although any rejection is a traumatic experience. We probably learn how to handle the trauma better as an adult but it always lurks in the background of any relationship. I could handle rough handling by members of my own sex but a casual, scathing glance by a girl was decimating. I could dream of asking some girl for a "date" but actually doing so was simply out of the question. I had nightmares of trying to do so and "wiping out and falling on my sword" by appearing like a tongue-tied rube with no social graces. Most are aware of the caste system that is present in India. Equally, most are horrified at the idea of any system like that in the United States.

In my mind a system quite like that in India was present, alive and well, right here. I always categorized the girls around me by a "caste" system and most of the girls that I admired I thought of as "much higher on the social chain" than I could ever aspire to be. I never had enough confidence, back then, to ask any of them on a date. Why would they ever stoop so low as to go out with the likes of me? I finally outgrew that feeling but it was much later on. I never thought about what the girls I actually asked out would have felt if they had known of my assessment of them as being "lower on the totem pole" like me. I'm sure that I was like a lot of other boys in that regard but that was no solace at the time. The answer to that problem was confidence, something that came to me much later. Confidence made life much easier and made me much happier. My personal confidence was drummed into me by the U.S. Navy. That was, perhaps, the best thing the Navy gave me other than the ability to fly their airplanes.

It was in junior high school that I discovered a latent talent. I found that I could accurately copy my parent's handwriting. More appropriately I could copy my Mom's handwriting, as my Dad took no real part in my education other than to threaten punishment if I didn't produce good grades. Whenever I had to stay at home due to an illness my Mother would always appeal to the same malady regardless of the cause. The note was always the same. "Please excuse Eddie's absence of (the date) as he had a sick headache and I kept him home". I always thought that the "sick headache" was a rather limp excuse and didn't really know just what a sick headache actually was but it always worked. I always thought that I could come up with a much more innovative excuse than that one. My Mom's excuses taught me that teachers really don't care about the excuses and probably don't even read them. The whole exercise is to see if the kid can, in fact, produce a written excuse. Thus armed I was ready for the next exercise.

One day I decided to skip school. I can't even recall the reason but a few kids and I had something more important to do than to attend school. Today I think that it had more to do with boredom than with anything else. We did so and, of course, were required to produce a note from home as a result. I wrote my own "excuse". I did so by copying an earlier excuse written by Mom and passing it off as the real thing. I kept the original excuse to use as a template. It worked and I was off on a new enterprise. Word soon got passed around that I was a superb forger. Kids who wanted an excuse written for some absence inundated me. I required no stipend. The notoriety was sufficient to satisfy my needs. All I needed was some sample of the kid's parent's handwriting to copy. I never had a failure. I believe, to this day, that I wrote some of the most innovative excuses the school had ever witnessed. True to my hypothesis I don't believe the teachers ever read the notes that I had expended so much effort on. It was a shame, in my opinion, that my best efforts were ignored.

My newfound enterprise came to an abrupt end when I skipped school for a week straight. I got away with it but was bored in the extreme. There was simply nothing to do. I found that I missed school and got tired trying to find things to occupy my time. The game grew old so I wrote my last excuse, posted notices that I was out of business and attended school like everyone else, possibly happier than most of the other kids for the opportunity to attend.

It was time to choose a High School. Flint had three High Schools at that time, Central, Northern and Tech. The first two were huge and were sworn enemies on the football field. Flint Technical High was very small and had a requirement for attendance. In order to be accepted to Tech a student had to have a "B" average in Junior High. I had opted for Tech thinking that a small high school would fit in with what I saw in myself concerning what I wanted from life and what I was willing to put up with. Tech emphasized scholarship and learning. It was short on flowery things like drama. It had an active sports program but one could safely navigate high school there without even acknowledging there were any sports. Tech didn't even boast a gym or an auditorium. It was perfect as far as I was concerned.

I left Lowell Junior High School without much regret. My new school would have no ethnic minorities threatening everyone with knives. I could concentrate on studying and not survival. I was happy.

Chapter Five

The summer between Junior High school and High school was uneventful. I could find no job for the summer that was lasting. Mom ragged on me unceasingly in an effort to motivate me to find a job but the simple fact was that there were no jobs available for young kids. It was 1949 and for some reason jobs were in short supply. I was too young to be employed by any of the major employers in the area. I tried to falsify an old birth certificate I had. I accomplished this by bleaching the birth date and inking in a new one but the first employer I tried that on, the Fisher Body Assembly Plant, caught on immediately. The kindly man interviewing me held the certificate up to the light and the alteration was readily apparent. He asked, "Has this been altered in any way?"

I was too honest to lie and disgustedly said, "Yeah, it has."

"Sorry son, but you're just too young to be employed by us. We have to live by the rules too. Come back in a couple of years and we'd be happy to hire you. Tell the next fellow you talk to that I said that."

I thanked him and left. Society seemed to conspire against kids. I always knew that. Why was I surprised? What the hell was I supposed to do for the summer? I decided to read and listen to classical music; the latter was something Mom couldn't stand.

The summer passed slowly and I'm sure that I was a real pain in the ass for my folks. I got fat and lazy doing all that reading and nothing else. Mom was unrelenting and tried to shame me into finding a job but an underage kid has all the cards stacked against him. I figured that it was all Mom's fault anyway. If I hadn't been thrust into a higher class a couple of times in the lower grades I wouldn't have been so young after leaving junior high. The law mandates that a kid has to be a bum and not work. It doesn't matter if he puts his brain to work also. Kids can't work and that's that. It's for their own protection, a term I loved to hate later on in life. You see, laws are made to even out everything. Laws are for the least common denominator. If some kid who was an underachiever made bad grades because he had an after school job then every kid had to be punished because of it. How does that stack up with the farm kids who worked their posteriors off in the early 1900s and still excelled in the little one-room schoolhouses in Middle America?

Eventually the summer waned and I got to go to High School for the first day.

The first day was memorable. I had been told that I would be hazed as a freshman newbie. OK. I was up to the task. I had been hazed prior to this several times and figured that it was just one more hoop I had to jump through. I entered the hallowed halls looking every inch the dumb freshman waiting to be plucked.

I got about fifteen feet inside the school when several older students walked up to me. "Well, what have we here. I believe this is a freshman. Are you a freshman, kid?" Kid. Damn! It was still with me. When would I ever grow up? Not "sir" like in Eaton or anything like that. Kid.

"Yeah, I'm a freshman. What do I have to do now?"

"Oh, that's simple. Just follow us and don't resist."

"I would be happy to do just that. Where are we going?"

"Right over here to the water fountain."

I followed them to the fountain and when we were arrayed there the seniors said, "Would you care to sit on the fountain or do we have to place you on it." My mother hadn't raised any idiots. I knew very well when to resist and when to go along. When rape is inevitable lie back and enjoy it, as the old, dumb saying goes. Why fight four seniors when you are going to have to get along in the school for the next four years? The fountain was an old fashioned type. It was made of porcelain and was of the bubbler type. When you turned it on it belched copious amounts of water; enough to satisfy the most dehydrated desert survivor. I willingly sat on the damned water fountain. I was thoroughly soaked when I was allowed to dismount. The seniors seemed very pleased with me and even evidenced admiration at the amount of water my trousers seemed to hold. The rest of the school day would be very uncomfortable.

Things went fine after the small hazing. Several seniors buttonholed me but upon seeing the masterpiece the first group had done on my trousers they allowed me to go in peace. I attended all of my classes and was happy with them. I was in High School.

Things went well for a few weeks. I had made friends with a Polish kid named John Kleinow and an Assyrian kid named Bob Lazar. I knew about Polish people but Assyrians were unknown to me. Bob explained his antecedents in the time-honored way that all Assyrians seemed to explain their heritage. "Do you know about the Medes and the Persians? Well, we aren't either one." I was a little confused by that explanation but it would suffice for the time being. We got along famously in spite of our varied backgrounds. We usually met early in the morning and ate lunch together at noon. We were a team. Then one day the inevitable bully cropped up.

One of the upperclassmen and two of his friends had formed some sort of an evil alliance. The friends were merely goons. They were the muscle in the equation with the head of the gang, Bob Octell, the ringleader. For some unknown reason they targeted me. One day, when I walked into the school, the three goons approached me and grabbed my books. They threw them down the hall and threatened me. "How d'ya like that, asshole? Want to do somethin' about it, prick? Want to do something about it?" With three upperclassmen just drooling at the thought that I might protest so that they could hammer me I thought, "Did my mother raise an idiot?" I assumed the stance of a brain dead three year old and allowed the goons to crow and raise general hell. Perhaps they were having a glandular episode. Maybe it would all go away. Who knew?

Eventually, as in all high schools, the bell rang and mercifully the goons scampered away laughing and allowed the learning process to continue. The next day the same thing happened. It seemed to be a trend. My friends were giving me a lot of room as a result. Who knew? Maybe the goon squad would notice them if they hung around me too long or too closely. Something had to be done.

Bob Octell lived no more than a block from my home. The next afternoon as I was making my way home from school my father drove by and gave me a ride. As we approached Octell's house I asked him to drop me off. He knew that something was up but wisely refrained from asking too many questions. He did ask if I needed any help. I was grateful for the offer but told him that I could handle it. When he let me out of the car I made my way to Octell's house and rang the doorbell. Octell's mother answered the door and informed me that he was at the local pool hall and wouldn't be home until late. Pool hall. It figured. I returned home and changed clothes to some dark trousers and shirt. After nightfall I made my way to Octell's house and asked for him once more. Again he was absent. I climbed up into a tree in front of his house, made myself comfortable and waited for him. Several times that evening I rang the bell on his door and asked for him. He was absent every time. Around one in the morning I gave up and went home.

The next morning I was met by the ubiquitous goon squad who asked me what I wanted to talk to Octell about. "Hey, asshole, you got something you want to tell us? You got a complaint? Why were you screwing around Octell's house yesterday? You want to be a tough guy? Let's settle this right now."

I remained calm as my books and lunch were tossed down the hall. I said, "What I have to say I'll say to Octell alone. It doesn't concern you guys at all." They blustered and crowed, threatened and flexed their muscles. I remained calm and quiet. It was apparent that they thought that I was thoroughly cowed. When they were through I retrieved my books and lunch and went on with my classes.

That evening my Father happened to give me a ride again. As we passed Octell's house I saw him weeding a garden. I asked my Dad to let me out of the car. He looked long and hard at me and finally said, "OK, but if you need help you know where to call." I told him that I knew and got out of the car.

I approached Octell at an angle that would not allow him to escape into the house. He looked up once and immediately went back to weeding furiously. I stood over him with my legs apart. "Do you know who I am?" He nodded without saying anything.

"OK, then, if you know who I am then you know why I'm here, right?" He nodded again careful to keep from looking at me.

"Octell, listen to me very carefully. I don't know why you and your goons are harassing me but it's going to stop right now. I know I can't fight all three of you and I'm not even going to try but I sure as hell can hammer you. You are going to be the target from now on. Anything that happens to me will happen to you. I don't care if I get beat up by some other guys or not. I'll beat the shit out of you each and every time I'm messed with and I'll make it hurt really badly. Whatever your goons do to me I'll do to you three times over. I've got lots of time and I mean every word. I swear I'll put you in the hospital. Do you believe me you piece of shit? If you don't then get off your fucking knees right now and let's have at it."

Octell never looked up once. When I asked him the question he nodded quickly without looking up. "Alright," I said, "Tomorrow starts your probation period. If I get hammered tomorrow you had better be watching over your shoulder every minute because it's going to happen to you. You can't hide forever. I'll get you sometime, somewhere. The longer I have to wait to get to you the more you are going to hurt. Hell, maybe you can even file for disability with your two broken legs." You can count on it." He nodded again. I left with my adrenalin peaking out. I hadn't touched him. He hadn't said a word. I had planned on simply tearing his head off but this seemed a better course of action.

When I thought about it I determined that I hadn't hammered him because he appeared so docile. Originally I was prepared to do my best to beat him to a pulp. What had happened to alter my course of action so drastically?

Some years later I studied psychology and the subject of aggression. One author had postulated that the reason why a lot of aggression is defused is because the victim assumes a completely docile posture. Think of the dog that throws itself on its back and urinates on its belly. That dog is completely defenceless at that time with its soft underside completely vulnurable. Normally the aggressive dog will simply sniff around and leave. The underdog is no threat at that time and does not need to be attended to. Perhaps this was the operative syndrome in the present instance. Who knows?

The next day as I walked into the school with my two buddies the goon squad walked up to me. My buddies peeled off expecting trouble. I expected trouble too but as the threesome approached they broke out into smiles. "Hi, Ed, How you doin'? How's it goin'?"

I was suspicious and frankly stunned. I fully expected to be hammered by the goon squad and I was fully prepared to break a few bones belonging to the ringleader, Octell. I stood stiff legged like a dog being sniffed by another dog while the three stooges patted me on the back and prattled nice things. My buddies couldn't believe it. When the stooges finally left for class my friends demanded to know what had happened. I related the episode that happened the last evening and they were ecstatic. Once again I had proven that sudden, draconian action will usually stun your enemy and the harsher and more innovative the action the more compliant will be the recipient of that action. I've never forgotten that lesson. And you, the reader, ought to never forget this little lesson in life also. It will make your life easier, more productive and a lot more pleasant if you can make any goon squad just go away.

Later on in life I read a treatise by Sun Tsu. It advocated the same action I took to solve my particular war.

And so I was in high school. Things went along just like for every other kid in high school. There were the usual heartbreaking love affairs, passing notes between classes to be read and worried over. The school was a technical school. One could choose a curriculum that advanced the student toward college or one that trained him toward a life of machine shops. I opted for a study involving the sciences. Instead of taking machine shop, pattern making and other hands on studies I elected Biology, Physics, Psychology, Metallurgy and Chemistry. I was fascinated by the sciences and even by economics but I only tolerated English, more's the pity.

One day I found myself in an English class that was composed completely of girls. I was decidedly uncomfortable there and especially so when the male teacher, Mr. Ellis, who seemed to prance about and simper, asked the students to write a paper about the meaning of love. The girls all tittered and shot glances at me while I slunk into my desk in mortal agony. Why was I subjected to this degrading class? All of a sudden the Dean of Boys appeared. He was a sort of Executive Officer for the school. Every male in the school liked and looked up to him. He took one look at the student makeup and said, "Edward, what are you doing in this class?" I replied, "Sir, I don't have any idea." He then said, "Come with me," and placed me in an all boy class much to my relief. I worshiped the man after that.

I had to take some technical classes since I was attending a technical high school. I opted for drafting and machine drawing. It seemed less blue collar than some of the other choices. The machine drawing teacher was a no nonsense, demanding, humorless man who was a very good instructor but not much fun. The students would work for a week on a drawing, take it up to Mr. Ammon for a grade and find him taking a small six inch ruler out of his top pocket remarking, "This doesn't look quite right". Inevitably the measurement would be off by a 32ond or a 64th of an inch and the long-suffering student would have to make it right before a grade could be assigned. I liked Mr. Ammon but I never saw him smile in all the years I was at the school. His infamous six-inch rule was well known and respected.

I had been taking Chemistry for some time. I had read more than was required by the teacher on the subject and one day I bet another student that I could make gunpowder. The bet was somewhere in the vicinity of one dollar. I mixed the appropriate amounts of charcoal, sodium nitrate and sulfur together and announced victory. My betting partner wouldn't hear it, however, and wanted to see empirical proof. I needed to burn some of it but didn't know just how to do it. Finally I scooped up a small amount of the mixture in the end of a glass tube and held it over a Bunsen burner. It worked just as advertised but what I didn't count on was the physics of burning gunpowder in an enclosed container. I had made an effective bazooka, a World War II weapon for shooting missiles. A long line of burning powder streaked across the classroom accompanied by shouts of "Look out" just as the teacher walked into the room. Unfortunately the powder trail pointed straight to me. The teacher, Mr. Jaquette, walked up to me and looked silently at me for what seemed to be a very long time. Then he turned and made his way to the front of the class and began teaching. Nothing more was said and nothing more had to be said. He had made his point.

The Chemistry class was the focus of a few more incidents in high school. It was taught by a very nice man, again, Mr. Jaquette, who knew what he was teaching and taught it well without embellishments and without talking down to his students. He believed in allowing his students to find their own level in the discipline. Every one liked him.

He used to get into trouble with the Dean because of his different methods of teaching. One day he allowed one of us, Jim Dagley, to bring in a .22 caliber rifle in order to demonstrate a physical principle of hydraulics, which was that a force exerted on a closed system was transmitted equally and undiminished throughout the system. He demonstrated this by allowing the student to shoot a cork into a bottle filled with water. The demonstration was spectacular as far as the students were concerned but the Dean was a little alarmed by the report of the rifle and when he investigated he found a classroom that was thoroughly wet with scattered glass everywhere. Needless to say he put a stop to that method of teaching. The students were on the teacher's side but all of our efforts were pointless. Can you imagine the panic in a school today (2008) if a student carried a rifle to school let alone shot it in a classroom? Different times, different attitudes.

Then one day Mr. Jaquette was cleaning out the chemistry lab, throwing items away that he felt he didn't need any more. Several of us were helping him as he was well liked and always had plenty of volunteers for any tasks he needed doing. We found a large jar filled with kerosene and containing a large chunk of sodium. Now for those of you who are not conversant with chemistry, sodium is a very active metal that reacts violently with water, hence it's storage in kerosene. We persuaded Mr. Jaquette to give us the sodium. Why he did so is beyond me but he did. It had been raining for a couple of days and everything was sodden. We carried the sodium out of doors on a piece of paper being very careful not to touch it as it would react with the sweat on our hands and burn us. We carried the chunk of metal to the nearest large puddle of water in the school yard and tossed it in. Now the puddle was, unfortunately, near a street and a stoplight. There were several cars stopped at the light and the occupants curiously watched us as we threw the metal chunk into the water. As soon as it touched the puddle it began to "smoke" and move violently around the water. As it generated hydrogen in its reaction to the water it began to explode in small bursts. The occupants of the cars were by now alarmed and began to get out of their cars. Suddenly a large bubble of hydrogen ignited and the sodium blew up with a loud bang. Small pieces of the metal hopped into the wet area and each exploded where they landed. It looked like a war zone. By now the car occupants were in full flight as they evacuated the area. The poor teacher stood in the large window overlooking the schoolyard saying, "Ohmigod" over and over again. The show was over in about five minutes but I'm sure that it went on and on with the teacher and the Dean.

Not to be undone by the episode of the black powder I made a bet with one of the students who did not value science that I could set a piece of metal on fire with one match. He, of course, didn't believe that I could do it so I stole a piece of magnesium ribbon from the chemistry lab. I met him in the machine drawing class and set out to win my dollar bet. I took a small piece of wood, split it and wedged the magnesium in it. Then I struck a match and held it under the magnesium. It ignited immediately and burned in the white-hot way that magnesium burns. It was about this time that the teacher came into the room. The boy I had bet with fled and I was left holding the burning magnesium that dripped onto the nicely finished desk. There was no way to put the burning metal out. Magnesium burns at a very hot temperature. Mr. Ammon, the machine drawing teacher, and I watched silently as the fire burned a large spot in the desk. When it was out he dryly observed, "You are, of course, going to pay to refinish that desk?" I acquiesced, "of course", and that was that. All in good time I was presented with a bill, which I paid in full, without letting my parents know what I had done. The cost of repairing the desk was several times the dollar I had won.

I used to eat lunch with Bob Lazar and John Kleinow. One day we were wandering around the school after eating. It was an old school with tunnels connecting it to another building that was used as a grade school. For some unknown reason Bob grabbed the fire alarm and set it off. We all ran as the strident alarm sounded and the schools emptied. I was angry and scared. Why the hell had Bob done an idiotic thing like that? The three stooges acted like we knew nothing whatsoever about the incident but unfortunately someone had witnessed the act and had told the Dean who immediately called us into his office.

"Boys, I want to know what happened and why. Anyone?" We all sat mute. It was, of course, the normal thing to do. No one wanted to tattle on anyone else. The Dean knew this, of course. After a few minutes of silence he said, "Alright, I'm going to leave you three alone for five minutes. When I come back I want to know just who set the alarm off." As soon as he left I said, "OK, Bob, you're going to confess. I'm not about to be punished for something you did and I'm not going to fink on you. John nodded his affirmation to the statement. Bob thought it over and finally did the right thing. When the Dean came back into the office he confessed. All three of us had a tongue-lashing and Bob had to write an apology to the fire department. That was it. I always liked that Dean. He was a fair but strict man. Anyone should be able to live with someone like him. I looked up to him and tried very hard to please him. I still think he was a great man. His name was Karl Mehring. I'll never forget it.

Mr. Mehring also taught a psychology class. I was in his class and found it fascinating. All of the books we had to read were furnished by the school system. At the end of the course we had to return those books to the school. They were supposed to be cared for during the time the students had custody of them and most of the kids did so without question.

When Mr. Mehring's psychology course was over and the time came to return the books one of the kids turned in a book that had been ruined by carelessness. The hard covers of the book had been ripped off and the book had been folded in half in order for the kid to be able to stuff it in his hip pocket. When Mr. Mehring saw the book he was upset. He lectured the kid at length and told him that he would have to pay for the book.

Prior to the book return I had asked Mr. Mehring if I could buy my text as I wanted to keep it as a reference book. He told me that there was no provision for a student to buy a book and that he was sorry but he had to refuse my request. After he had taken the student who had ruined his text to task Mr. Mehring called me to his desk and gave me the ruined book. Then he warned the kid who had ruined his text not to ask me to pay him for the book. I now had my reference book but the kid who had ruined the book was not very happy with me. No great loss. I had and always have had a love for books and still have no regard for those who don't.

One morning I awoke with a toothache. It began with just a little pain but it wouldn't go away. Mom sent me to a dentist who practiced locally. He said that I had a molar that needed to be removed. Fine and dandy and easy to talk about but this was 1950 and dentists were closer to the time when teeth were removed with bullet molds than modern day dentists. The dentist numbed my jaw and began. The tooth apparently was stubborn and refused to come out easily. The dentist struggled and ended up putting his knee against my head in an effort to gain a little more leverage. The tooth finally gave up the struggle along with what seemed to me to be a lot of blood. Eventually everything worked out OK but I had a gaping hole and a dull ache in my jaw for a week or so afterwards. Thank God for modern day dentistry.

John and Bob were my buddies at school but after school hours I had two others who lived closer to my family's home. Their names were Jim Dagley and Jim Evans. All three of us loved firearms and shooting. We used to shoot our .22 caliber rifles almost daily.

Sometimes we fired in the country in a series of glacial moraines that offered a very nice backstop for shooting. Sometimes we shot in a local range and sometimes, especially in the summertime, we would go to a local garbage dump and shoot the rats that frequented the dump. 22 ammunition was cheap then and we used to burn up hundreds of rounds a week. I think that the going rate for a .22 round was about one cent. We could buy a whole box of fifty for a half of a dollar. We became very good marksmen, no one got hurt and everyone kept out of trouble. Young boys today could profit by the same activity, as could society. We learned respect for firearms, marksmanship, and responsibility by shooting, both on the ranges with adults and by ourselves in the country. It was a wonderful time in our lives as we bonded with each other and learned respect for weapons and each other.

One day all three of us were firing on a range maintained by the William's Gunsite Company, a world renowned outfit. All of a sudden two small heads appeared atop the large dirt backstop that served to protect items downrange from stray bullets. I called attention to that and an adult began to scream, "Cease firing! Cease firing on the firing line!". Everyone did, of course, and the man called down two small boys, about twelve years of age, who had somehow entered the range by the back side, had climbed the firing backstop berm and were looking at the shooters in the line of fire. Luckily no one was injured but it was a sobering experience for both the shooters and the Williams Gunsite Company.

My family had relatives who lived near Detroit. Specifically I had a cousin named Ira there. My parents used to visit our relatives often and it was nice to see my cousin and interact with him. He was more adventurous than I was and in later years would give his parents problems because of this. He always had more interesting things to do whenever I showed up and it was pleasant to try and keep up with him. In the winter we would line up near an intersection where the street had not been cleared by a road plow. We always picked an intersection that had a four way stop sign on it. When cars would stop at the intersection we would crouch down behind the rear bumper and hold onto the bumper so that when the car started up again we would be drug along on our heels. It was heady sport and sometimes we could attain close to thirty or forty miles an hour on our feet before letting go. Dangerous? I would say so, but then dangerous things attracted boys. Sometimes one of us would wipe out but the other boy would usually be able to grab the one who had fallen and was able to drag him until the car stopped at the next intersection.

During the summer time we would go to an old gravel pit where we could board any of several rafts that had been constructed by kids out of old wood salvaged from any place available. The rafts were precarious at best and several times I boarded one only to find that its best attribute was to sink once it was in the open water. Again it was heady excitement. There were always several rafts available in the water. Most times I could hop from the one I was on that seemed to be sinking to another one that seemed to be afloat. Life back then was wonderful and none of us could be harmed in any way, or so we thought.

High school was a nice time in my life. I liked the challenge of learning, I got good grades and I learned many new and wonderful things. I didn't resist the learning process as did some others and sought out the sciences instead of the manual arts. I valued learning and reading above all else.

The Biology class was a favorite of mine. It was taught by a funny little man named Harry Hammond. He had very short legs and was cross-eyed. As he explained to the class, he wasn't really cross-eyed but instead only one of his eyes would focus at a time. The other one wandered. He was very fair and a good teacher to boot. I was only one of two males in the class as the technical curriculum mandated biology only for the female sector of the student body. Most of the boys bypassed the biology class for classes in machine shop and metallurgy. I was an aberration in the biology class. The girls seemed to be embarrassed by my presence. I was embarrassed by theirs. I felt like an outsider in the class but was interested enough in it to stay the course. The teacher seemed to know how I felt and liked the fact that I wanted to learn what he taught. The girls didn't matter. Who cared what they thought anyway? One day after a test the teacher tried to tell the class how he graded. He had a unique method of grading. He assigned grades not on a standard or a curve but on what he thought your aptitude was. He told the class how he graded and told them that someone like me (he singled me out) would have to do much better than the "average" student in his class since "I was capable of doing more than the average". It made me feel very proud that he thought that I was a cut above the average but it also made me wonder if I was being discriminated against for some reason. It really didn't matter in the final analysis since I got an "A" for the course.

Mr. Hammond invited me to attend a nature course for a week at a local camp that was given for students from all three high schools in the Flint area. The camp was situated in an area that was full of glacial moraines or hills that were made when the glaciers covered our country. It was the same area where my friends and I spent hours shooting. It was a wonderful experience and I learned more in that week than in any other in the whole semester. I spent time with a trapper, learning the customs and life styles of several indigenous small animals like fox, skunk, and others. I went on field trips learning about the local trees and shrubs. I made friends with another student from another school who was a Golden Gloves boxer and I used to accompany him on runs when he would use a jump rope to keep time with his footwork. I was eaten alive by mosquitoes and covered with poison ivy but I loved every minute of it. The experience suited my love for the out-of-doors and nature in general.

I hated English like most of the other males in the school. The English teacher, Ms. Caulkins, was a cold lady with halitosis who had no sense of humor whatsoever. Her students, all males, had plenty of humor, however, and exercised it whenever they could. Usually that humor was wasted on the teacher and only the students appreciated it. It became de rigueur for anyone in her class to hold his nose any time Ms. Caulkins leaned over him to correct his writing. Her bad breath was phenomenal but, since no one possessed the courage or the incentive to broach the subject to her we resorted to jokes at her expense instead. English seemed to come naturally to me. I didn't have to study at all and in all of the tests I answered the questions in a way that seemed to make sense to me. I can only give the credit for that ease to my Anglo-Saxon parents who spoke English the way it was supposed to be spoken. I usually got Bs in most of the tests and that seemed good enough. As a result it was late in life before I could even define terms like perfect and pluperfect. The term reflexive was entirely foreign to me as was subjunctive.

One day one of my classmates brought into class a small box of Borax. For the uninitiated, Borax crystals introduced into nasal passages will produce a series of explosive sneezes. The small crystals were quickly passed around. As the big hand on the clock hit 45 approximately 20 students quickly sniffed a crystal or two. In seconds the classroom was bedlam as 20 students all exploded into sneezes simultaneously. The sneezes were obviously real as was the interruption. The teacher knew that something was awry but didn't know what it was. Inquiries directed at individual students produced shrugs and the plea, "Gee, I don't know. I just had to sneeze." It was all part of the educational process for both the teacher and the student and it had the wonderful side of being humorous, an attribute that is given short shrift today.

I found an after school job in a small grocery store on the southern side of town. It was a very good job for a young boy but I had to take a bus from school in order to get to work. The bus ride was about a half an hour trip and I had to walk about a half mile after that. The storeowner was an old Jewish man named Jack Diamond. He was a jewel in the rough. He was kind and caring but you wouldn't know it if you didn't know him. He was mostly silent, preferring others to do the talking. He lived above the store in a comfortable apartment with his wife. His children were both in college at that time.

I did anything and everything he asked me to do. I put up stock, dusted, arranged the stock, cleaned the meat cases, carried out groceries for people who needed help and did a myriad other things requested of me. The pay was fair and always on time. What could be better?

Jack Diamond had another employee. I knew him. He had been a classmate of mine a long time ago in grade school. He was always a spoiled kid. He had anything he wanted and lorded it over those of us who were poorer and had less. He was my first introduction to those people who are elitists, who feel that they are better, much better, and worth a lot more than the "common" people. Needless to say, I didn't care much for him but I am capable of getting along with most people whether or not I approve of them. (Editors note: I'm much less able to do that now that I'm at an advanced age.) Oh! Did I mention that he was also a braggart? He was a thoroughly unpleasant person.

I didn't see much of him as he worked after I did. One day our work schedules overlapped. He motioned for me to accompany him into the beer cooler. When I followed him he dropped his voice to a whisper and confided that he had a problem. His problem was that I was working too hard and too fast. I was making him look bad, according to him. I listened silently as he explained his grand plan. We were both to work a lot slower. That way the storeowner would have to use us more thus paying us more. What did I think about that?

I finally told him that I thought his plan was flawed. He wondered how. I said that I liked my job, liked my boss and was willing to give a good days work for my pay. I considered him to be a conniving, lying, no-good cheat and I wasn't willing to go along with any plan he would ever concoct. Did he wish me to explain any further? He was stunned. He wasn't used to people denying him things. Did he wish any thing else? No, he didn't. "Fine," I told him, "Stay out of my life in the future, OK?" I left him in the beer cooler where he belonged. No doubt he became a politician in later life.

It was usually dark by the time I got home since the store was at the exact opposite part of the town from my home, and then I had to do homework. Even with all of that I figured that my life was good. I had a good home, was attending a good school, had a good job, had spending money and had a girl friend. What more could a kid wish for?

One day while I was walking from the bus stop to work a car pulled up and honked at me. I waved to the guy in the car and he motioned me over. I was friendly and trusting. I approached the car and the man inside said, "Get in." I saw no reason not to and did so. He started driving and talking. I thought that he was a customer that I hadn't remarked on previously and wanted to give me a ride to work. When he asked me where I was going I became suspicious. Every time he spoke to me he would reach over and pat me on the leg. The pats became more frequent and higher up my leg. I sidled over to the right side of the car as far as I could. I told him I wanted to get off at the store as we approached it. He wanted to know what time I got off work and I lied to him. I told him eleven O'clock. The store closed at nine. He seemed happy with that and I left the car. My hackles were raised and my whole body was in the flight or fight mode. I had finally figured the guy out. He was "queer" and he had tried to pick me up. I felt degraded, angry and wanted revenge. I always carried a jack knife and planned on how I would deploy it in order to do battle if he approached me again. I never saw him again but filed the whole scenario away in case it ever happened in the future. When I told my father about the episode he smiled and said, "Do you know what you would do if it happens again?" I told him that I had given it much thought and figured that I could account for myself in an OK way. He nodded and left the situation to me. Today (2009) any kid caught carrying a jack knife would be prosecuted, kicked out of school and ostracized. Kids today cannot protect nor defend themselves. Have you ever called 911 and watched the clock to see just how long it takes the police to respond if they even do? Have you ever timed just how long it actually takes to dial 911? Do you always have access to a phone? Do you think that a pedophile or a child molester would wait until some frightened kid could get to a phone and dial 911? Think about that in terms of a kid without access to a telephone and who is set upon by a pedophile. Think about the fact that the police are, as one friend termed it, "historians" and can only react after some crime has been committed. Food for thought.

In the summer Jack Diamond asked me if I would mind weeding his wife's flower garden in a slack time. I told him that I was happy to do so. His wife was a pleasant lady who told me that her irises were not blooming like they should. I inspected the garden and told her that they were far too overgrown and needed to be split. She had no idea what I was talking about so I dug the whole thing up, split the bulbs, replanted them and weeded the whole area. She was very happy and the next year had a profusion of flowers. Jack was happy because his wife was happy so everything was well.

One day a small, fast talking man entered the store. He didn't wish to buy anything. He wanted to talk to Jack Diamond. I was stocking shelves and couldn't help overhearing the conversation. The man was trying to generate money for the new state of Israel. He pleaded with Jack for an hour, imploring him to help his people in their time of need. Jack remained immobile and inscrutable as always. The man almost turned himself inside out in his pleas for money. Jack remained silent. Obviously Jack didn't wish to contribute. This was really a high-pressure sales technique. I had to admire the man and had to give him an "A" for effort. Jack also got an "A" for resistance. It was fascinating to witness. The man pled, hammered his fists on the counter, stamped his feet, turned in circles and generally worked his body in remarkable ways in order to drive home his points. Finally Jack rang up a "no sale" on the cash register and handed the man a ten-dollar bill. He quickly closed the register as the man threw the ten dollars on the floor and stamped on it. "Jack," he screamed, "I'm not going to accept that. I'm only going to accept hundreds of dollars. Jack, Jack, this is for your people. Think about what you are doing, Jack. You are casting your own people to the wolves. How can you do this, Jack? How can you face yourself? I would be ashamed if I were you. I'm ashamed to even be talking to you with this attitude, Jack." Amazing! I was impressed. I'm not now nor never was a salesman. This guy was a super salesman. As good as he was Jack remained implacable. Finally the man left empty handed. I was proud of my boss. He was one hell of a defender. He personified a Chinese philosopher I read much later on in life when I was studying karate. He said something like, "In order to conquer one must overcome his opponent. In order to defend one must merely survive." Jack was a survivor all right.

Jack had a problem. A small child of approximately ten years of age began to hang around the store. He would yell at all of the customers saying, "Don't go into that store. It's run by an old dirty

Jew." It was embarrassing, to say the least. It wasn't hard to figure out where the kid got his attitude problem but Jack didn't feel like calling the parents and complaining. This was 1951 and people generally figured that you needed to solve your own problems instead of running to the police or hiring a lawyer. I knew that and felt sorry for my boss. The kid finally resorted to entering the store and yelling, "Dirty Jew!" at Jack. Jack, stoic as always, tried very hard to ignore him. I couldn't and didn't have to do so. Pretty soon another kid about twelve years old came in to buy some candy. I buttonholed him and asked him if he wanted to make five dollars. His eyes got big and he nodded that he would love to make big money like that. I told him if he would beat up on the kid in front and send him home bawling I would give him five bucks, cash. He left immediately and we were treated to a lot of yelling and scuffling followed by a lot of bawling. The kid I had hired came triumphantly back into the store and I gave him five dollars and thanked him. Jack watched the whole episode silently. When it was all over he walked silently over to the cash register and rang up "no sale". He extracted a five-dollar bill and silently handed it to me. I accepted it and he smiled. I was proud of having solved a very vexing problem. I had never heard of the Mafia, strong-arm tactics or anything else concerning mob tactics. I simply did what I felt was necessary and expedient. Jack was a fine person and didn't deserve to be treated in such a manner.

While waiting on the bus to go home one evening I witnessed another episode of cruelty and power much like I saw when I was a small boy. Another boy approximately my age was walking with his girl friend when two larger boys made some lewd comments concerning the girl. The boyfriend took exception to this and challenged the two, unwisely I thought. Obviously one of the two larger boys had some prior experience with fighting. He immediately took up the challenge and smilingly beat the boy to a pulp. It was a "no contest". The girl refused to stay around and walked away from the fracas. After the boyfriend had been beaten properly the goon squad actually shook his hand as if this was some sort of a deal or game. The boyfriend ran off after the girl after he had shaken the hand of his tormentor who walked off laughing with his friend. Obviously this had been a planned scenario and both tormentors knew in advance how the whole thing would end.

I thought about the episode a lot. There were a lot of lessons to be learned here. The way I figured it the first mistake the beaten kid made was in not choosing his battles. This was an unwinable battle as far as I was concerned. If the beaten kid won in the first foray then the larger of the two tormentors was obviously there to chip in and ensure a victory for the two goons. One side had a backup and the other side did not.

The second lesson was that victory was paramount if you really wished to win in a fight. Rules were secondary if they figured in the equation at all. The beaten kid had a choice. Did he wish to win the battle or did he wish to follow the "rules" or what everyone thought he should do and get beat followed by the victor shaking his hand. I would have picked up the first weapon I could and slammed the aggressor. Screw the rules. Forget them. This wasn't the fighting ring. This was the street. You could get hurt on the street.

Then there was this matter of shaking hands. Later on in life I would witness a bevy of lawyers who were trying to destroy a person wanting to shake his hand as they were introduced to him. What a farce! Why would you want to shake hands with an enemy? What stupid rule dictates this aberration? None of us were Knights of the Round Table. I vowed that I would never shake hands with an enemy. There are some basic rules that apply if you wish to survive. They could be listed as Landers Rules of Engagement and numbered. As an example:

Do not allow an enemy to feed you or give you anything to eat.

Do not allow an enemy to take care of any wounds you might have incurred.

Do not allow an enemy to think that he has pulled the wool over your eyes and that you now think of him as your friend.

Do not follow advice from your enemy.

Do not believe anything your enemy tells you.

Do not believe people who come from the enemy's side who say that they are your friend and want to run interference for you in order to allow you to become friends with your enemy.

There are numerous corollaries to the above Lander's Rules but they would be too numerous to mention here. The Rules were added to as time went on and at last count were somewhere in the order of 3568. Enlisting in the military and becoming a Naval Aviator later on in life added to the Rules immensely. In military terms most people could be categorized into one of three distinct groups, hostiles, friendlies and neutrals. One could only relax around the friendlies.

I worked for Jack Diamond for several years. I liked the work and loved my employer. He was a very fair and kind man albeit a taciturn man. I always felt comfortable with him and regretted the occasion when I had to leave my employer.

Girls were a problem. I didn't have much money and had no car, as did some of the other, more affluent kids. I always felt like the "kid across the tracks". I asked a number of girls out on dates but all of my dates had to be transported where we wished to go via public transportation, usually the city bus. I felt like a second-class citizen and wondered why any girl would ever accept a date from me when they could accept a date from one of the "fast" kids who had access to cars and lots of cash. Thankfully for me there were still a few girls who had some old fashioned ethics and who valued a poor kid like me who seemed to value girls for who they were and not what they were or what you could get from them. I used to listen to the "fast" kids who bragged about their conquests and told every one about the girls they had "bedded". I figured that about 90% of those reports were false and were more the figment of the "heroes" imaginations than anything that really transpired. I felt sorry for the girls who were taken in by the flash and the show of the popular kids. They were usually discarded by those kids later on and had to live with the results.

I sort of kept track of all of the "popular" kids that I knew in junior high school. Most of them did not excel. Most of them were punks in later life just as they were punks in junior high. They were the ones who never excelled; the ones who did the drudge work in later life. Some of them I felt sorry for. Some I thought deserved the life they created for themselves. Watching them I felt like an alien looking at human interaction on a strange planet. They used to affect me but in later life they didn't count for anything in my life at all. It was a sobering lesson.

I've always believed that all of the efforts to educate those among us who simply don't wish to be educated is a complete waste of time and treasure. People like that ought to rightly be allowed to seek their own level. If they wish to become trash then so be it. The current political correctness idea about education is doomed to fail. It has resulted in the dumbing down of the system and the waste of time, effort and money on kids who simply don't want to learn. Kids are not allowed to fail any more. They are, accordingly not allowed to learn in that they never realize their shortcomings and are not allowed a corrective proccess. More attention is allotted to their "egos" than their brains. This is, most likely the result of a Socialist government interferring in the learning proccess. Kids in the old one room schoolhouse used to get a better education than the kids today in plush school surroundings.

One day a kid who lived across the street from us invited me into his house. He wanted to "show me something". What he wanted to show me was his father's handgun. The kid had found out that his father had a Walther P-38 in his dresser drawer. He led me to his Dad's bedroom and took out the gun. Then he pointed it at me and said, "I could shoot you right now if it was loaded". I objected to his pointing the gun at me and asked if I could "see" the weapon. When he gave it to me I jacked the weapon open and found that it was fully loaded with a full magazine and one round in the chamber. All he would have had to do was to pull the trigger and I would have been one dead cookie. I was extremely angry with him and told him so. He couldn't figure out why I was so upset. I never had anything to do with him in the future. He was stupid beyond measure.

My father had become the pastor of a tiny church in the north of the city. When he accepted responsibility for the church it only had about four families trying to support it. They could be considered to be among the poorest of the cities families but were nice people and good as gold. Dad spent most of his time trying to build the church population and was successful to a point. The church added a wing and the population grew. I was proud of him but he was a driven man and wasn't happy with his results. One of his problems was that he didn't see people as people. His congregation all had faults of one sort or another and he couldn't accept that. He took all of their problems on his own shoulders thinking that somehow he was at fault and had let them down. He became more and more reclusive and dictatorial. He actually drove some of his congregation away with his draconian ideas. In his world there was no gray, only black and white. Finally he left the little church and accepted a position in another very small church in another village. That church wasn't as successful as the one he had left as the area was less populated and, being populated with German farmers, they were either Lutheran or Catholic. Now my father would have no congress with any other belief systems believing that they were aberrations and not really Christian. He called them all "isms" and dismissed them outright. He was not what you would really call an easy man to get along with. In his world you were either a Baptist (Southern variety) or you were relegated to the masses he considered atheistic.

Dad believed implicitly in the King James Version of the Bible as it was written. Literally. If the Bible said the world was created in six days then that was it. I once asked him where the dinosaurs fitted into the Bible and he immediately accused me of being a "heathen" and allowed that I should fall on my knees and ask for forgiveness for asking the question. Since I didn't exactly see things his way I was watched with suspicion for some time.

I was, I guess, a rebel. You could probably make the case that I still am a rebel. I decided, about this time, to explore other faiths rather than simply accept the Southern Baptist version of how things worked. This, of course, immediately placed me outside the family's inner circle. My father barely spoke to me. I didn't care. He seemed to be a very gloomy preacher, postulating hell, fire and thunder to his congregations. I didn't want to hear it. I went to as many churches in the city of Flint as I could find, usually with my buddy Jim Evans. All of this exploration didn't solve any real questions but I did rub shoulders with a lot of people that I never would have experienced otherwise.

One Sunday evening I attended the services of a Negro church. It was uplifting and different but when the time came to pass the collection plate the pastor made a little announcement. He said, "We sort of expect more of an offering from the white folk among us since they all make a lot more money than we do. The Lord looks favorably on those who give more so you white folk, please dig a little deeper. Amen?" The congregation all mimicked "Amen". Jim and I couldn't get out of there quickly enough. We didn't have all that much cash among us and pretty well emptied our pockets, saving only enough money to get us home on the bus. I guess the pastor figured that we were there for entertainment and could damned well pay for it. Maybe he was right.

I rubbed my father the wrong way as I thought that worship of the Lord ought to have a little more decorum than the Southern Baptists offered. I tended to like the services of the Episcopalians, Lutherans and others who had a more formal service, a little more quiet service, one that gave you time to contemplate and reflect. Dad didn't see things that way. I probably contributed to his eventual breakdown as he most likely considered me just another one of his failures.

I was never comfortable with girls. I guess that I always considered myself to be somewhat a bumpkin, never smooth and comfortable around girls. Lots of my contemporaries dated girls and, according to them, had many episodes of sexual encounters with them. I was appalled. My religious upbringing prohibited me from ever trying to entice any girl into a sexual liaison. I couldn't envision doing anything like that. Nevertheless, I had the same urges and hormones, as did my contemporaries. It made for a very interesting time. Due to my shyness and reticence in trying to date the girls in the church that I attended, the First Baptist Church of Flint, Michigan, painted me with the emblazonment of "uncooperative". I always wondered why I was stamped "Uncooperative". Perhaps it was because I didn't particularly like any of the girls that were in the "Young Peoples Group". Who knows? At any rate I was an outsider; something that

I was familiar with. I didn't care what the "young peoples group" thought of me. I was my own person.

I used to listen to the radio on Sunday afternoons. Television at that time was pretty boring and mostly static and snow. The radio was an old standby. The station I listened to was funded by Colonel Robert McCormack and was an opera station. My mother used to tell me to "listen to it in my room as no one wished to hear the caterwauling that was what most opera amounted to". Accordingly I listened to the station in my room. Sometimes (OK, most times) I missed the Young Peoples meetings due to listening to the operas. It was a personal thing. I'd rather listen to the opera than the wet, repetitive crap that was spewed by the wonderful leaders of the young peoples groups. I had heard it all before and was tired of hearing it again.

One day the doorbell of my home rang. It was Sunday afternoon. My father answered the door and saw a company of young people from the First Baptist Church who were "concerned". They were invited into our home by a beaming and approving Pastor Landers and seated. They danced around the subject for a little while and then cut to the chase by explaining that they were concerned that I might be "feeling ill or something" because I had not attended the young people's meeting for 6 weeks in a row. My father mugged for the group, shaking his head and clucking over his "wayward" son. He called me into the room and asked me, in front of all of the "young people", why I had not attended the meetings. I thought, "Shades of an Amish community. Am I going to be shunned next?" I tried to explain how I would rather listen to an opera than attend the mushy, pretentious young people's meetings but this was met with stony silence. Obviously no one in the room was on my side nor did they wish to hear any alternatives to the wonderful little group that they had formed. I was a definite threat to them. Dad assured them that I would be counseled and they left mollified. I was disgusted. What ever happened to the recognition of hypocrisy? At any rate I was permanently stamped with the banner of sinner, uncooperative heathen, backslider and any other name that they could think up. I didn't care. The issue had been resolved. I didn't feel like I had to hide my intentions any more and I could listen to my operas in peace. I've never forgotten that the leader of the group that showed up on my doorstep was a classmate at Flint Technical high school named Bill Barger. He became a preacher in later life and much later contributed an article to a book I authored that told the stories of the classmates of mine that attended Flint Tech. As I read Pastor Barger's biography I was reminded of the edicts against the sins of pride and boasting the old biblical heroes talked about and I couldn't help but think, "I knew it all along". I do believe that it also says, somewhere in the Bible, "Judge not, least ye be judged". Later on in life I used to occasionally watch a TV show called "Confrontations". It was all about confronting drug addicts and alcoholics. As I watched it I flashed back to the "confrontation" I had in my own home by the Young People's Group from the First Baptist Church led by Barger. It always makes my hackles stand up.

One of the girls in the First Baptist Church didn't find me repulsive at all. She attended the same high school that I did and generally got in my way until I finally noticed her. Once again, I had been chosen and was only too happy to comply with anything the lady wished. We exchanged notes in the hallways of the school, made cow eyes at each other, held hands when we thought that no one was noticing and generally did what any high school kid of that time did. That is to say we didn't rent a motel to shack up, get drunk or high on drugs, shoot any peers or run off to some foreign country and get married like modern kids do. We decided to pledge undying love for each other and I, for one, thought that this was the end of any love affairs for me for the foreseeable future. As any kid in his teens is prone to do my emotions were topped out, as were my hormones. The governor on the whole situation was my religious upbringing that seemed to nag at me reminding me of my obligations to family and the other party in what seemed to be my love affair. I had stark fears of bringing disgrace down on myself and my family along with the girl in question. Ranked against those fears were the raging hormones any teenage kid possessed. Nice!

One Sunday those hormones and feelings topped out when my new amore allowed her hands to wander over to my crotch area during the morning sermon while we were seated in the balcony of the Baptist Church we attended. I was appalled. What in the hell was I to do? Sometimes we had to stand to sing the hymns listed to be sung. Standing was a problem with a male with obvious male sexual reflexes. I could only try to drape my jacket over the obvious sexual exhibition my girlfriend had given rise to. My upbringing told me to move away and have nothing to do with the girl. My emotions told me to, well; you can probably figure that out for yourself. This very emotional issue was something that plagued me for some time. It was finally resolved by the girl in question telling me that she had figured out that I had become more of an issue for her than the Lord and, accordingly, she would have nothing more to do with me. That was that. How can you argue with the edicts of the Lord? It occurred to me that perhaps she had tested me and that I had come up lacking somehow. Perhaps she was looking for someone who would "cooperate" just a little more than I obviously had. None of this cogitative thought did anything to alleviate the very real mental agony I experienced due to this rejection. It was only the first in several rejections by the female of the species, normal for a teen-age kid. As odd as it seems I usually agreed with the reasoning given for the rejections. Most of them made perfect sense. None of them ever soothed the fevered brow of the cast off male in question. This particular rejection was a very saving occurance as the logical result of the continuance of the relationship most certainly would have been an unplanned pregnancy as was the case for several of my high school friends. I had dodged the bullet and didn't know it.

We had, by now, moved from the north of Flint to a nice old house near to the center of the city. It was the first house I think my family bought. Prior to this they had only rented houses. The house was comfortable with two stories. I had my own room, as did my sister. It was a heady experience, a far cry from the little farmhouse in St. Charles with no central heat, no inside water and an outdoor privy. The house had an old coal-burning furnace called an "octopus" because of all of the large ducts jutting out from it and leading to large grated holes for the transmission of heat. It became my job to break up coal for the furnace in the winter. It was a small enough price to pay for coming up in the world.

Now families that had more money than my family did owned furnaces that were called "stokers". They bought coal that had been broken into small chunks that was transported to the furnace on a conveyor belt that was integral to the furnace. It was an easy system designed to keep the furnace furnished with an unlimited amount of fuel at all times. I always considered those families "rich". Our furnace burned the same type of fuel but number two or three coal was much cheaper than stoker coal and so we bought number two or three. The coal we bought consisted of chunks of anthracite that could be as large as two or three feet in diameter. In order to get the coal into the furnace I had the task of splitting up the large chunks. I used both a pick and a sledgehammer. It was dirty, hard work. When I had broken up the large chunks I had to shovel the coal into the furnace. During the winter months the furnace had to be attended to at least twice daily. On colder days I had to tend it more often. At night I had to "shake down" the furnace. That task made the ashes and cinders, the unburned chunks of coal refuse, drop to the bottom of the furnace. Sometimes the unburned or partially burned coal would coalesce into a hard, unburned chunk. Those pieces of unburned coal were referred to as "clinkers" and had to be broken up in order to get them through the gratings in the furnace. The breakup was done by me and was hot, dirty work. I then had to shovel out the ashes and put them into a metal can to be carried away by the trash collector. I'll never forget the smell of those ashes. It was the exact same smell I remembered as a small kid growing up in Terre Haute, Indiana in 1936.

The old house had a wonderful perk in the form of an old claw foot bathtub. The bathroom (there was only one) was on the second floor and was spacious. I soon found that the absolute, best way to relax was to run that old bathtub full of hot water and immerse myself up to my nose in it. I even found a metal tray that fit across the tub that allowed me to place a book on it and read while I baked and soaked myself. There was nothing better than jumping into that tub in the winter and becoming red from the wet heat of the water while I engaged in my favorite activity, reading. It was the best item in the house.

My mother washed clothing in an old fashioned washing machine. It incorporated a tub that contained a washing agitator and a "wringer" that consisted of two cylinders driven by the machine. The washing was accomplished by separating the clothing by color, washing the separate loads, wringing them of the soapy water via the wringer and depositing them into a tub containing cold clear water. You then had to rinse the soapy water out of the clothes by hand and wring the water from them using the wringer again (it swiveled to allow you to do this). You could gather up the load to be hung out on a "clothes line", a rope strung across our back yard where the clothes could dry in the open air. In the winter the clothes were hung in the basement or the kitchen. Once again, the smell of wet, drying clothing will always be with me just like the smell of coal ashes. One had to be very careful of the wringer. It was easy to catch your hand or your sleeve in it and be drawn into it to be "wrung", a painful process. There was no safety release. Mom insisted that I learn how to do the washing and the ironing. She wanted me to be able to be independent. I'll always thank her for giving me the basic values that I have carried with me throughout my life. I can take care of myself, thanks to her.

Mom also taught me basic things that kids everywhere ought to be taught but are rarely instructed in today. Things like simple words like "thanks", "please" and how to wait for people to exit an elevator before entering it. You know what I'm talking about; the small things that make society run a lot more smoothly. I was taught to take my hat off in an elevator, to offer a lady or an older person my seat on a crowded bus, to hold a door open for the person behind me and not to interrupt anyone while they were speaking. I'm appalled by the lack of common courtesy on the part of people today.

At that time there was no liquid soap for the washing. I used to pare off small pieces of Fels Naptha soap to be placed into the old washer. Fels Naptha was a large bar of cheap soap. The soap pieces would dissolve in the hot water and would wash the clothes.

Fels Naptha was an ugly brown color and had a distinctive odor. I'll never forget that either.

The clothesline was a unique and humorous institution. There were a series of cotton rope lines strung across our back yard. They constituted a hazard for those who didn't know they were strung there and could possibly become "clothes lined" if they ran across the yard at night. In the winter Mom dictated that the wash be hung out immediately after the final wringing. They became immediately frozen, of course, and were as stiff as a dead cat. They were gathered up and brought into the large kitchen to thaw out and dry completely. I used to argue with my Mom about why we had to hang them outside in the first place but "the wash" was done according to custom and couldn't be altered. Arguing with Mom was futile.

The winter hazards of the clothesline weren't the totality of the humorous aspects of the system. In the summertime the clothes would flap in the breeze as they dried. `The family dog saw the flapping clothing as a fine target for "fetching" or "catching". Mom would try to keep a weather eye on the wash in order to try to keep the dog from jumping up and catching a shirt in his teeth. From the dog's point of view it was impossible to ignore the flapping clothing. He used to leap up and catch a shirt and then just hang there by his teeth. The backyard would erupt in a bevy of flapping from Mom flapping her arms to the clothing flapping in the wind to the dog simply flapping as he ran from Mom. It was chaos in color, and it was wonderful.

Ever heard of a clothes prop? A clothes prop was a long piece of lumber that was notched on one end. The notch went under the clothes line and served to keep the wet wash off of the ground as the line would sag under the weight of the wet washing. Clothespins were made of one piece of wood that was split into two "legs". The "legs" kept the clothes fastened to the clothesline. Later on clothespins would morph into two pieces of wood that were joined with a piece of wire that served as a hinge. "Pinch" type clothespins were much more effective than the old one-piece type. Monitoring the clothes props was my job also.

Our wonderful old house had a front and a back porch. The front porch had a few chairs on it so you could sit and watch the foot traffic pass by. It was the custom, then, to say "hello" to anyone passing by. It was a nice custom and was only slightly altered in the south by the people saying "hey" instead of "hi". People used to sit on the front porch in order to relax in the evening. Things were a lot more relaxed back then. The neighbor who lived next door was an old man who enjoyed sitting on his porch and watching the world go by. I used to sit and listen to him recount his days as a young boy in the early Flint, Michigan days when the area was a lumbering center. He recounted tales of the new cut lumber being floated down the Flint River to the market to be turned into boards for building. He was fascinating and we spent hours enjoying each other's company.

The back porch was a battleground; at least it was in my family. Dad had somehow acquired an old hound dog named Susie. He had images of Susie putting up bevies of quail, rabbit, partridge and pheasant. Susie had other ideas. She was what dog breeders call "intact", in other words, she had not been "fixed" or neutered. Susie had ideas of raising a family. One day she came in estrus. Dad didn't pick up on this but every male dog in the whole county did. We were soon inundated with male dogs all wagging their tails in an effort to get in good with the humans who could allow Susie come out and play. Dad did his best to try to convince the massed dogs that Susie was a virgin and couldn't participate. He was totally unsuccessful.

Dad's order of battle was to line up a series of coke bottles interspersed with an old iron and a broken toaster on the banister that lined the back porch. He would hover in the kitchen so that he could peer out of the back window. One day when I had gone over to my folk's house to visit, Dad gave me a cup of coffee but refused to leave the kitchen. He kept jumping up and looking out of the back window. Finally he yelled, "There's that S.O.B. again." He ran out of the kitchen onto the back porch grabbing any of his missiles that were close at hand and firing them indiscriminately at a target in the back yard. I ran out onto the back porch in order to battle whatever terrible enemy Dad had identified only to find an old hound dog who was intent on courting Susie. He had easily leaped over the back fence and was engaged in leaving the yard in the same way. He apparently didn't harbor any grudges and was even wagging his tail. He only wished to make the acquaintance of the lovely female dog in our yard that was also wagging her tail. Neither dog understood exactly why Dad was upset and trying to hit the male dog with a coke bottle. I shared their confusion. I asked Dad why he didn't simply put Susie in the garage until her condition improved. It was like arguing the Scopes Monkey Trials all over again. Dad figured that the male dogs could damned well do what he dictated. His family had been raised to do that so why couldn't a dumb dog do it? I tried to point out that the dog was dumb and that was why he wasn't ever going to win this fight. He wouldn't listen. I left figuring that he would go on into eternity throwing coke bottles at male dogs who could not understand why they were being put upon any more than Dad could understand why the dogs didn't see things his way. Oh, and by the way, you must realize that coke bottles back then came in distinctive green glass bottles and not in plastic ones. Glass bottles have a much more satisfactory trajectory when thrown than do plastic ones.

Susie eventually became pregnant and I used to tease Dad about a virgin birth since he was ever watchful and made sure that all of the male dogs were kept out of the back yard. Her litter of beautiful puppies was abundant and Dad managed to give all of them to people who were caring so everything worked out OK.

Susie had another fault besides the obvious one of being female. She loved to tip over the garbage can and sift through the contents. She would especially watch when a fresh offering was placed into the can. She would then tip the can over as soon as the human had disappeared into the house. None of her faults included being dumb. Dad despaired at ever being able to teach her to cease her obnoxious ways. He finally consulted me. I solved the problem by attaching a firecracker to the next load of garbage and lighting it just prior to fitting the garbage can lid atop the can. I then hurried into the house and watched out of a window as Susie lifted the lid just in time to have the firecracker go off. She never repeated the act again; in fact you couldn't get her within five yards of the offending can.

Susie was originally bought by Dad for the purpose of hunting. Susie, of course, thought that raising a family was paramount, but hunting was inborn in her and, as such, she was a good hunting dog. The problem was that Dad didn't know just what Susie would hunt. That attribute would surface later on.

Chapter Six

The garage on Dad's property stood unattached and separate from the house. Dad didn't keep any of the family cars in the garage but had configured it as a warehouse since he had accepted a position as a salesman for the Jewel Tea Company. As such he had a route he attended with a company furnished step van that doubled as a moving super market. The garage was used to store all of his stock.

There was a significant crack in the back wall of the garage. Dad ignored it. I tried to tell him that it was a harbinger of bad things to come but he ignored me too. I was used to being ignored but the crack in the garage wall didn't see things exactly that way. The crack was ignored for years. One evening I got a call from Dad. He said that there had been an explosion near his house. I got in the car and drove over to see what was happening. When I got near his house I saw nothing but emergency lights in the street. There were fire engines and police cars all around his house. I was apprehensive and hurried to the house. Dad met me with a sheepish grin on his face. He said that he had called the police and the fire department about the "explosion" and they had responded quickly. The emergency people fanned out to try and find the source of the explosion. Finally Dad said that a policeman with a huge grin had knocked on his back door and said, "I think I know where the explosion came from." Dad followed him to the garage that had simply given up the ghost and fallen down. The "explosion" was the walls of the garage falling.

Needless to say the garage was a mess. The neighbor lady was especially miffed since one wall of Dad's garage had ruined her bed of Irises. She stood with her arms crossed and watched the efforts to correct the ruined bed of flowers. One of my favorite pictures was the one I snapped of Dad standing in the ruins of his old garage, grinning as he picked over the debris. Dad didn't let "things" bother him. "Humans" bothered him. Get him out of the mess with people interacting as people do and he was happy. His calling as a pastor was not conducive to happiness.

Things finally came to a head when my Father broke with reality. His church had not been a happy institution for him. Attendance was down and the congregation seemed to not wish to follow his leadership. Dad took that as a sign that he had failed as a leader. He dropped into depression.

My parents had been having problems for some time. The evidence was apparent and the flags were flying. I had no idea how to address their problem and they tried heroically to hide it from me. Finally it came to a head whereby I couldn't ignore it any longer and they could not keep me out of it any longer either.

I had gone to bed early and was sound asleep when my Mother came into my room and shook me awake. "Eddie, you need to go see your Father." I was groggy and asked why I needed to "see" him. "Never mind, just go down to the basement and see what you can do," she said.

I reluctantly got out of bed and made my way down to the basement. When I got there I found my Father with a shotgun. He was trying to lever a shell into the breech of the gun but was unsuccessful because he had consumed a large quantity of alcohol of indeterminate identity and was, in layman's terms, as drunk as a skunk.

"Dad, what are you trying to do?" I asked. All of a sudden I was wide-awake.

"I'm trying to shoot some rotten son-of-a-bitch." Dad was slurring his words and he was obviously upset about something. I suddenly became very wide-awake. I had been taught from the time that I was a little boy that you didn't load nor play with guns in the house. My father had taught me those rules. Now he was violating them.

All of a sudden it dawned on me that he might have been trying to commit suicide. He had been depressed for some time. No one knew how to treat depression at that time. We simply figured that he would snap out of it some day. Then the straw that broke the camel's back happened. My mother found a friend that made her happier than my father did.

Dad suspected that he had a competitor and investigated until he found evidence, which he confronted Mom with. She confessed and he started drinking. The whole episode culminated with me confronting my Father in our basement with his shotgun. This was serious. I didn't know whom he intended to shoot with the gun but it was obvious that he intended to shoot someone. Another serious problem was that a drunk man with a loaded shotgun is an accident just waiting to happen. You never knew just what would happen and neither did the drunk. This was serious. I had to do something. I grabbed the stock of the shotgun from behind Dad and pulled the gun away from him. Then I ran like hell out of the basement into the back yard. As I did I threw the gun under the back porch. Dad ran after me bellowing. He was serious and would have hammered me if he could catch me. I ran around the house and ended up in the dining room where I grabbed the telephone and tried to call the police. I dialed the operator (there was no 911 then) and tried to explain to her what my emergency was. I think that I had found the dumbest operator the telephone company had hired. She refused to connect me with the police department and kept trying to ask me a lot of questions. I finally shouted, "Damn it; get the police out here right now. This is an emergency."

Dad finally caught up with me and I dropped the phone and fled. Dad grabbed the phone and listened to it for several seconds. Then he pulled the phone out of the wall, snapping the phone cord and severing the connection. He threw the phone across the room and continued his pursuit of me. I kept the dining room table between my Dad and myself. We circled the table a couple of times with Dad shouting for me to give him back his gun. I refused. He threatened to break my neck. I told him that I could whip his ass if he tried and he was drunk enough to acknowledge that I probably could which would have, under other circumstances, been humorous. We circled the table until the front doorbell rang. I ran over to open the door and saw two of the largest humans I had ever seen. They were the response unit to a domestic disturbance. I invited them into the house. They entered with caution. I learned much later on in life that domestic disturbances were the bane of the police units that had to respond. I related the whole incident to them and they began to question my Dad. He readily confessed that he had tried to load his shotgun but was very vague about just why he was trying to do so in the basement and in the house. The police finally determined that Dad was too drunk to make much sense and, because his son, me, had preferred some charges on him they took him in custody along with all of his weapons and most of the big kitchen knives. I always thought that it could have been humorous, under the circumstances, that the cops took all of the kitchen knives along with Dad since he was now gone and no one else presented any threat to the family.

We all slept fitfully that night. The family was in turmoil. Dad was in the pokey and his family was distressed about his actions and their own in making it possible for him to spend the night in jail. We discussed the incident at length and finally determined that Dad needed help in the form of head shrinkers, otherwise known as psychiatrists.

Two days later Dad was released from the county jail and I picked him up. He was distressed about his guns. I could relate to his distress but was very worried about him trying to commit suicide. He kept asking about his guns and I kept telling him that I would release the guns from the county police when I was sure that he was lucid enough to accept them. He had to enter a program of examination and treatment by a psychiatrist as dictated by the court system. Two days later I took him to the local headshrinker and was told that I could not stay with him. He had to undergo a session of electro-shock. When I picked him up he was only able to slobber. It looked to me like he was brain-dead. I asked a lot of questions but the "headshrinker" would not answer any of them citing the "patient/doctor relationship. I told my mother my misgivings about the whole thing but she was sure that the "doctor" was right. The electro-shock treatments went on.

I dropped my Dad off and picked him up from the witch doctor for two months. Every time I picked him up he looked like he was abnormal. I was distressed about the whole thing. I asked the doctor about my father's treatment but got only evasive answers. I didn't have much to say about any treatment relative to my parents as I was just the "kid" in the family and had no legal status at all. Still, it seemed to me that the so-called "treatment" smacked of something right out of the 1600s with the "aberrant people" being thrown into snake pits. I didn't like it and, as time went on, I liked it less and less.

Much later on I would minor in Psychology in college. The main idea I got from my studies was that the discipline was not only a "new science" as it was advertised, but was more appropriately accomplished with feathers, drums, dwarfs and a lot of smoke. In other words, it was not far removed from the hypothesis stage of the scientific procedure. I've never respected the so-called science and I probably never will.

My father finally came home much more docile and a lot quieter. Wouldn't you be quieter if a substantial number of your brain cells had been fried? I think that I liked him better the way he used to be. I can, in retrospect, make anyone act the way my father acted when he came home, but no one would like the methodology. In the early 1900s it became very popular to have a prefrontal lobotomy performed on one's self in order to become "more relaxed and calm". For those of you who do not know just what a prefrontal lobotomy is I submit the following. The procedure was accomplished by inserting a slim knife under the eyelid and into the brain itself. The knife was then manipulated from side to side in order to destroy the frontal lobes of the brain, the main centers of higher thought and ideas. The result was that the "patient" became very docile and quiet, not at all concerned with the normal things that would bother normal people. Neither was the "patient" ever concerned with any type of higher thought like economics, politics, art, music or religion. The concept of actually destroying one's brain never entered the equation. I did not concur with the protocol but then I was not consulted.

When Dad came home he was very concerned with the disposition of his firearms. I didn't blame him. I had some firearms also and would have not wished anyone to confiscate them. It left one with a feeling of nakedness and helplessness. I have always felt that possession of firearms is equal to a feeling of freedom. I'm sure that Dad felt the same way. Without the means of protecting yourself how can you feel truly free? Irrespective of any feelings anyone might have had I felt that, considering the propensity of Dad to shoot someone (I always felt that he was referring to himself) it was advisable to have his guns placed somewhere where he could not access them easily until he had proven himself. The police were very cooperative and would not release them until I said for them to do so. Dad used to beg me, on a daily basis, to get his guns back. I felt for him but wanted a little more time to pass in order for him to prove himself.

About a month later he got all of his guns back and we never had any more episodes like what happened to us that night.

Dad settled down to a life of introspection and living a normal life, at least a normal life in terms of how life was lived in the 1950s. He took up hunting, which was fine with me. I loved to hunt. I hated to shoot any animal or bird but loved to fire my shotgun or rifle. I readily agreed to go hunting with him any time he wanted to go. It was a catharsis for both of us.

We hunted pheasants, those slow-flying, heavy bodied imports from China. It wasn't much of a challenge. Sometimes we headed north to hunt partridge. Now that was more like it. We walked through heavy woods seeking to flush a partridge or two. When they flew up they invariably startled you as they waited until you almost stepped on them before they flew. Usually I would shoot a tree or two as the canny little birds would dodge left and right around the trees. I always was sorry when I shot one, as they were very game and could fly and dodge better than any game I had ever hunted. It seemed a shame to shoot a bird that could outthink you.

One beautiful fall day we decided to go hunting locally in the Flint, Michigan area. We decided to hunt rabbits and took Susie along to scare them up for us. Susie was enthusiastic but ineffective. She followed her nose along any and all trails she found. We finally gave up and decided to allow her to have fun while we hunted. We were having a good time when it occurred to me that Susie was baying a lot. It sounded like she had something treed. I alerted Dad to her noise and we began to track back to see where she was. We soon found her. She had ventured out on the ice of a fast flowing river and had broken through the ice and fallen in the water. She was hanging onto the ice and baying for help. Dad was very upset. He could see his dog freezing and dying right in front of his eyes.

I grabbed my .22 caliber rifle and yelled, "If I can break her free from the ice she's hanging on to she will float downstream to a place where we can grab her and haul her ashore." I opened fire and chopped a circle of ice away from where she was hanging on. She went under the water when the ice broke away but popped right up again and was now in the little circle I had made. There was no way she could get into the free flow and float down to a position where we could haul her out.

I watched the poor dog get weaker and weaker as the cold water sapped her strength. Dad was ineffective and only yelled a lot. Finally I said, "OK, I'm going to shoot her. I'd rather do that than let her freeze to death." Dad threw a fit and yelled, "Don't you shoot my dog." I could relate to that and asked him what the hell he wanted to do to save her. He finally said, "Maybe we could find a branch that we could use to scrape her off of the ice and onto the bank." That sounded like a plan. We hunted around and I finally found a large branch that had fallen off of an oak tree. I hauled it over to the area and between Dad and I we managed to pull Susie out of the water and onto the ice. We then scraped her over the ice and onto dry land. She was pretty well immobile by this time due to the cold. I grabbed her and ran to the car, which was sitting in the sun. The inside of the car was very warm. I dumped Susie into the back seat and covered her with a blanket. Dad and I continued to hunt, bagging three rabbits. When we came back to the car Susie was in the backseat, alive and well, wagging her tail and asking to hunt once more.

There was one more hunting episode that I remember with disgust. Dad and I had gone to the more northern areas of Michigan in order to hunt deer. We were part of a party that consisted of a few men from Detroit who considered themselves to be hunters but who had not even touched their rifles in over a year. One of the Detroit men had fired at a deer and had only grazed it. I saw the deer running and fired at it, hitting it in the head area. As the group converged on the hapless deer it tried to hide and bleated with a piteous noise. I felt terrible about the fact that it was not a clean kill and levered another round into the breech of my rifle intending on administering the coup-de-grace to the deer.

Dad kept me from doing that, insisting that the person who had originally shot the deer was the "owner" of the deer and could do what he wished with it. As the fat person who had originally shot the deer ran up he huffed, "I need to stick him". By that he meant that he needed to cut the deer's throat in order to bleed the deer.

I argued that the deer needed to be shot again in order to put it out of its agony. No one would allow me to simply shoot the deer again. The "hunter" who had originally shot the deer pulled his hunting knife out and slit the deer's throat. As the deer died it actually drowned on its own blood. Not a smooth death as in a quick dispatch from a rifle bullet.

As I watched with disgust the "hunter" flipped the deer over on its back and attempted to field dress it. I said, "Better to leave it alone until it's dead". No one paid any attention to me. The so-called owner of the deer continued to attempt to cut the deer's belly and suddenly the deer died. Its hooves cut a merry pattern on the "hunter's" hands as the flight or flight movements of the dying deer took effect. I was happy watching the "hunter" dress his cut up hands before he "dressed" his deer.

The "great white hunter" then cut open the deer's gut and pulled out the intestines. He happily announced that he had dressed the deer. The deer's diaphragm was readily apparent as a shining white piece of flesh. I disgustedly took out my hunting knife and cut the diaphragm allowing the lungs and the heart to fall free. The Detroit hunter didn't know what to make of the "additional" internal organs. He said, "Where did all of that come from?" I vowed from that time never to "hunt" with another dumb big city hunter again.

Dad was more of a normal person now and I could cease to worry about him. Now I could worry about the normal things that a kid worried about while growing up.

It was about this time that my mother began to have some health problems. After several trips to the doctor it turned out that she had tuberculosis. It was advanced and wasn't helped at all by Mom smoking as much as she did. Finally she was advised to enter a TB sanatorium for treatment and we accomplished this with much grief. Luckily there was a sanatorium in Flint so we could visit her whenever we wished. It was strange being without a mother to look out after the family. We didn't ever appreciate how much she did for us all until she was absent and we had to shift for ourselves. I include Dad in that assessment. He seemed lost. Everyone chipped in and we all coped but not as well as if Mom had been at home.

Mom was always the glue that held the family together. I suspect that Moms all over the world are the same. It may even be that Moms in the Islamic world occupy the same niche. Who knows? In any case the Islamists are too stupid to acknowledge that fact since they exist primarily in the Stone Age.

Dad was lonesome so whenever he could get the time off he and I went fishing. Now I could take fishing or leave it alone but I pretended to love it so that Dad could have some fun. It was nice to have a father so close so I had no complaints. We used to plan the fishing trips so that we would be on the lake of choice before sunrise as Dad figured that the time frame was optimal for catching fish. The way we did it was to go to a drive-in movie first.

Now I realize that the reader might not know just what a drive-in movie is all about. It was a very popular sport during the 1950s. It consisted of a very large screen with a big parking lot in front of it. At periodic intervals in the lot a number of posts were placed. The posts had a speaker on a long cord attached to it. The idea was to pay for each person in the car, drive to a post where the occupants wished to view the movie, park and hang the bulky speaker on to one of the windows of the car. That way everyone could both see and hear the movie in the privacy of the car. There was usually a concession building in the center of the complex that housed restrooms and places where the hungry could buy popcorn, soda and candy.

Drive-in movies were very popular with the younger set. Kids would try to beat the system by hiding several of their members in the trunk in order to minimize the number of tickets they had to buy. When parked the trunk would be opened and the kids would all pile into the car to watch the movie free. Older kids would choose the movie in order to neck and "make out" in the privacy of the car during the movie. In cases like this the movie was secondary to the primary purpose of accomplishing whatever sexual activity could be coaxed from the person in the passenger's seat.

Dad and I would attend a "double feature" movie, sleeping through most of the boring parts. When the movie ended it was just in time to drive to the lake of choice, get the boat ready and be on the water as the sun rose. We would fish until about noon or until we were disgusted by the lack of fish caught and would then retire home to nap until late afternoon. It was a lazy and satisfactory life. My sister was old enough to get herself ready for school so she was taken care of until late afternoon. We spent one whole summer this way.

Mom had to undergo an operation to remove part of her lungs. She spent about a year and a half in the sanatorium and was pretty much an invalid when she was allowed to come home. It was a happy occasion when she returned. Things returned to normal even though the rest of the family still had to pick up the household choirs. By now we were used to it so things were fine.

Early on, even before Mom went into the TB sanitarium I was required to help out around the house. I learned how to cook, clean, wash and iron and was required, on a regular basis, to accomplish all of these tasks without supervision. By the time she was able to come home the house could pretty well run itself. Mom had always mandated that I learn how to fend for myself so that I would never be dependant on another person for anything. I've always been grateful to her for teaching me all of those skills as I've used them throughout my lifetime. Mom had a unique way of teaching things one needed in order to survive around a home. She would patiently teach the procedure whether it was cooking, cleaning or ironing and then assign tasks for me to accomplish. It was to my detriment if I slacked off or shirked any task, as corporal punishment of some sort was sure to follow. Mom did not believe in pussyfooting around when it became obvious that a heavy hand was required and if she didn't think that she was up to the task then there was always my father to stand in for her and take up the slack. Mom also had some unique ways of reinforcing her teaching methods and imparting recurrent training. One day I was given the task of making a pot of butterscotch pudding for the evening meal. I knew that milk would quickly burn if it was being heated and was not constantly stirred but for some reason I left the pot and busied myself with something else. When I returned the milk was burned and the resulting mess was inedible. Mom took one look and pronounced that I would profit by having to eat the whole pot thereby remembering for all time the lesson to attend to heating milk. I've never liked butterscotch pudding after that and I've also never forgotten the lesson. I can still remember the taste of burned butterscotch pudding. It's something you never forget.

Reading had always been a great resource for me. Books were as precious to me as anything I could think of. I read anything I could get my hands on, books, magazines, encyclopedias, even the dictionary. I envied the kids whose parents could afford the National Geographic magazines and thoroughly enjoyed any visits whereby my parents took me to a friend's house where I could find those wonderful publications. Early on I had answered an advertisement that had asked if I was interested in the Book of Knowledge, a set of encyclopedias. Of course I was interested. It didn't matter if I was only eight years of age and had no worldly assets. I was definitely interested. I didn't take my mother into my confidence so she was surprised one day when an encyclopedia salesman showed up to sell young Eddie a complete set including the mandatory yearbooks extending into the next century. Mom was a real sport about it and swallowed the salesman's pitch with the result being that our household soon owned a set of that exalted fountain of knowledge. Within a couple of years I had read the whole set from cover to cover. I've always considered the two major attributes toward attaining knowledge to be an inquisitive mind and the ability and love of reading.

The summer Mom was in the hospital was a busy one. Jim Dagley, Jim Evans and I were inseparable. Dagley and I attended the same high school while Evans attended another. In spite of this we managed to get together just about every night after school and homework was done and we declared war on a colony of Norway rats that had infested an old garbage dump left unattended in the country. Shells for our .22 caliber rifles were cheap back then. We would buy a couple of hundred rounds each, load up Dagley's car and drive to the dump in the evening twilight. Once there we attached flashlights to the rifles, loaded the magazines, turned off all lights and waited. Soon the rats would appear, scampering over the discarded tin cans and miscellaneous garbage piles. When the noise of the rats had increased to a level that indicated a large number of them the flashlights were turned on and used to target individual rats, which were then shot. To us it sounded like a war zone.

To those of you who think this sport was inhumane I submit that a .22 caliber, long rifle, hollow point bullet usually meant instant death to a rat. The small town that owned the dump was happy that we had decided to do away with a noxious problem and there was always the added problem of actually hitting your target at night by flashlight especially when the target was moving fast and turning constantly. Nevertheless we chalked up an impressible score of kills by the end of summer. By the next spring, of course, the number of rats had actually increased. Later on I would come to know this was called a "target rich environment".

When the weather turned too cold to comfortably shoot rats Jim Evans and I turned to swimming as a diversion. Jim had joined the swimming team in his high school and I had always been good at the sport so we tried to swim each evening at one of the local public swimming pools. The pools were heavily chlorinated and as a result our eyes were constantly bloodshot from the chemicals.

Swimming and marksmanship thus were cultivated very early in my life. Both skills were very advantageous later on when I joined the Navy and became one of the military brethren.

High school was a happy time. I either held my own or excelled in most of my studies. The only problems I encountered were social ones. I didn't feel very comfortable with the opposite sex and, as my situation in life was on a lower socio-economic scale, I felt rather inadequate around my peers. Well, they were really never peers since I never had enough "stuff" in the form of personal possessions like clothing or cars like they had. I never felt a lack of things until it came to the vexing problem of asking a female out on a date. It always seemed that everyone had more opportunities and personal possessions than I ever could hope for. Most of this was more perceived than real, of course, but then most of life is all about perceptions rather than reality. Perception becomes reality for most people as they react to what they think they see and what they believe is real. Two people will see the same thing differently and act in divergent ways depending on their perceived assessment of the situation. This was how I reacted to my perceived lack of social status and my meager wardrobe.

If my social life was lacking my studies more than made up for the deficiency. I had no interest in working with my hands and so I tended to avoid the "shop classes" that were offered by the Technical High School I attended. I took only those shop classes that were mandatory, classes like Pattern Making and Machine Shop. I found that the sciences were much more interesting and so I opted for Biology, Psychology, Physics, Chemistry, Metallurgy and all of the math classes I could sign up for. Since these classes were more heavily invested in credit hours than the shop classes were I accumulated many more credits toward graduation than my peers did. Now it must be recognized that I did not do this out of any preplanned long range strategic goal. Like most things in my life it simply worked out that way.

I've long wondered why I didn't study Chaos Theory and esoteric math like that since it has always seemed to me that things happened to me rather than being planned for or thought out. I think that, for a life as chaotic as mine has been, it has been an overall success and very interesting in the bargain. It has been far more interesting than anything I could have ever planned for and argues for a higher power that exercises some oversight in regard to my life.

In my final year of high school I had determined, for unknown reasons, that I had enough credits to graduate early. Why I even added things up is beyond me and can only be explained by the previous paragraph. Chaos operating in a vacuum. Eureka! I had finally found the finish line. I imparted this jewel of information to my buddies and was roundly jeered as trying to accomplish the impossible. Everyone knew that one didn't graduate from high school early. You could always simply quit if you were old enough. Some of my peers had proudly done just that, leering at those of us who were so disadvantaged as to have to stay in school. Thus speaks ignorance cubed. Those unfortunates who were left considered themselves to be put upon because they had not flunked enough classes in order to be able to be old enough to quit. Again, later on in life I learned that the word "quit" was an anathema and that the word "persistence" was worth gold.

In order to prove to my peers that I was right and they were wrong I requested an audience with the Dean of Boys in my school. This gentleman was a very polished and learned man who took his mandate of teaching, leading and counseling his charges very seriously. He already knew me from my attendance in one of his Psychology classes. When I appeared in front of him he smiled cordially and said, "What can I do for you, Edward?"

"I want to graduate early."

Dean Mehring chuckled and said, "Oh yes, you and about fifty other boys in this school."

"I mean it, sir. I've got enough credits to graduate right now. I don't see why I can't do it."

"Well, Edward, that's impossible. You can't have accumulated enough credits to graduate early. Look. I'll show you." He walked to a file cabinet and opened it. Thumbing through several rows of files he extracted one and carried it to his desk. Opening the file he perused it casually and then, becoming more interested, he looked closer. "I'll be damned," he whispered.

"How did you do that? Did you plan that?"

"No sir. I just took the classes I wanted to take. I don't like shop so I took the more interesting classes. They are worth more."

"Yes, I can see that and I can see what you took as electives. Well, you are correct. You technically can graduate early but the question is what are you going to do then?"

Well there, he had me. I didn't know what I was going to do. I had never considered what I would do after high school. Wasn't it enough to just graduate? My mother had graduated from high school but my father had not done so. All conversations around my home had revolved around whether or not to graduate and there had never been one word spoken as to what one did after the fact. I was stumped. What did one do after high school? Kids were supposed to follow in their Dad's footsteps and do what he did in order to put bread on the table. Wasn't that the big plan? How did one do that? On the other hand, why would one want to do that? How did one go about finding a job? What was out there for me? All of these questions ran through my mind in an instant. Good question, Dean. What was I going to do? I had honestly never considered it. My life, up to this point, had amounted to fifteen years. Was I prepared to go out into the big world and make my way? I had read all of the books like Toby Tyler and how he ran off to join the circus. It was a delightful story but I wasn't naive enough to think that I could do some thing like that. I thought about the question and finally offered the standard "kid" answer.

"I dunno."

"That's what I thought," the Dean answered. "Well, the answer to your question is no. I'm not going to allow you to simply waste your life. You need to stay in school."

Again I thought long and hard and finally offered the stock answer found in every kid's repertoire, "But it's not fair."

The Dean snorted, "Edward, fair is what I say is fair. I'm not going to turn you out on the world knowing as little as you do. Have you ever thought about higher education, about college?"

College? In my family graduating from high school was considered the epitome of all educational processes. College was for other people. College was costly. Collage was for the rich and gifted. Who had the wherewithal to attend a college? "Dean Mehring, my family doesn't have enough money to send me to college and never will have. No, we haven't thought about it at all."

"What if you didn't have to pay for college? Would you consider it then?"

"Well, sure, but who would pay for my college other than my folks?"

"There are numerous ways of going about something like this. The only way I would consider allowing you to leave high school early is if you entered college. Would that be alright with you?"

College. To my knowledge I would be the only person in my extended family to ever enter a college, whatever the credentials of that bastion of higher learning and socio-economical scale. I loved learning. Why not continue doing so? I had no plans for the future. I had no plans for the present. I had no plans at all for anything. It didn't take much higher cognitive thought for me to tell the Dean, "Sure, why not?"

Dean Mehring nodded to himself and picked up the telephone. He pointed to me as an indication that I should stay in my seat. Since he was the Dean and second only to God I had no problem whatsoever in obeying him. He had a short conversation with someone outlining my scholastic history after which he sat the phone down and simply looked at me for what seemed to be a long time. Then he said, "OK. It's pretty well set. Come back to my office tomorrow at lunchtime and we'll start processing the paperwork.

Meanwhile I've got to contact the Registrar at the college and set this up. Now get out of my office!"

"Jeeze!" I thought. "He's pretty touchy this morning. All over a little request to leave school early!"

By the end of the next school day I had accepted an agreement from the Flint Motor Freight Scholarship Foundation that stipulated that I would receive tuition expenses as long as I maintained an A-B average in grades. In addition I was now signed up to study at the Flint Community Junior College. My father, who had never graduated from High School, thought that this endeavor was extraneous nonsense but my mother thought it a wonderful opportunity. Dean Mehring had said that he had some misgivings about the whole affair but that he wished me well in his new quest. "Don't make me regret letting you go early," was the last thing the Dean had said.

I started college the next week. I still had two high school classes I had to take in order to be accepted to the college but wise heads allowed me to take them concurrently along with my college classes. Since a high school was within walking distance from the old college my classes were scheduled there. I took a math class and a physics class in high school along with English, Math, Chemistry and Speech classes in college.

The college was held in an old insane asylum. It was a spooky series of buildings connected by underground tunnels, which the students used in commuting from class to class. I felt at home in the old buildings but I was, once again, out of my league in terms of age groups. I was the youngest kid in the whole college and I felt it acutely. Girl friends in college were out of the question. What budding college girl wishes to be associated with a high school kid? My only friends were Korean War Veterans who were trying to catch up with the world and were attending college under the G.I. Bill. I grew up in a hurry.

My studies took up most of my time so I neglected all of my old high school buddies. My only associations were with the vets in my college classes. I learned a whole new vocabulary along with a new bunch of values, mores and attitudes. In the infrequent times I got together with my old high school buddies I found that we were pretty estranged in attitudes and vocabulary. In short, I had outgrown them in spite of not wanting to do so.

One day I wore a new shirt to college that I had bought. It was the newest thing in high school fashion. It was a pink, V-neck T-shirt. I thought that it was a great shirt until I attended my first class. One of my vet friends came up and said, "Gee, Eddie, why don't you get a nice little flower to wear in the V part of your delicious shirt?" He affected a lisp as he said it and all of the other vets laughed uproariously. I went home at the first opportunity and threw the offending shirt in the trash.

My new "buddies" who were, by and large, mostly Korean War veterans, had lots of stories and tales of their life in that foreign country. I learned of the cold, the fear and the hunger of the common dogface soldier who had to exist there. I learned that they were mostly unanimous in turning down an offer to go to officer's school and become a "thirteen week wonder" or, in other words, a new Second Lieutenant. They told me that the life expectancy of a new Second Lieutenant was about three weeks as the Korean snipers looked for them in order to kill them and demoralize the rest of the platoon. I learned about all of the various jobs the vets had. It was an intensive and heady education for a young student. It did the exact opposite that the vets figured it would. Instead of turning me against the military way of life it made me want it all the more. God, it was exciting. I was used to the regimentation already, having been in the Naval Reserve for some time. It seemed that the regimentation was the one thing that united the vets against the military way. I didn't mind that at all. The challenge of that way of life appealed to me. It was certainly something to think about.

Soon it was time to "graduate" from high school. Since I had nothing in common with my old school buddies I elected not to attend the graduating ceremonies. During the ceremonies I was awarded the high school's Bausch and Lomb Science Award. Obviously I was not there to accept the award so it was mailed to my home along with a disproving letter from the Dean castigating me for my non-attendance. The next day I proudly told all of my Korean War Vets about my new honor. They were initially enthusiastic about my honor and asked me how much money I had won. I had to confess that there was no money involved and when I did my new friends were caustic in telling me that "Jesus, Ed, if there's no money then why are you bothering us with this story? It's meaningless." I was disappointed by their disapproval but understood that, in their terms, money was the only meaningful measure of approval. It was another eye-opener.

Ed. My newfound friends had called me Ed. That was the first time I had been called by that truncated name. Before this I had been Eddie. Welcome to the real world. Howya doin' Ed? Howzit goin'? What's it feel like to grow up?

I listened to the stories of these vets over coffee between classes and learned a lot about the real world and how it works especially during wartime in a war zone. By the second semester I was not a high school kid by any measure of the term. I had grown up a little bit.

About this time in my life I had purchased a little lot near a nice lake around the middle of Michigan. I had spent a summer there and found it a very nice, peaceful place. There were just a few people living there at the time. They were unpretentious and friendly. I liked the place.

The summer that I graduated from high school a school chum, Maurice Cummerford, and I decided that we would camp there for a week. We planned the trip and put together tents, food and whatever we thought that we would need. Dad furnished the transportation. The place was about a two-hour drive from Flint on Lake Wixom, which was really the backwater of the Titabawassee River. The lake was miles long.

We arrived near the river's dam in the evening and in short order had our tents pitched, food stored in trees to dissuade any roving bears and a nice fire going. Dad wished us well and shoved off. We lazed around and finally turned in. The next day we did the usual kid things in the woods, cleaned up the camp and became immediately bored. We finally decided to hitchhike back to Flint, call our girlfriends on a pay phone and hitchhike back. We figured that would take all day and then some. Now that plan might sound pretty idiotic to the reader but please bear in mind that you are undoubtedly older than sixteen and undoubtedly a lot smarter. There is nothing more dangerous than a bored sixteen year old.

We got to Flint in a timely manner, called the girls as planned and started back to our camp. Hitchhiking in the evening was a little different from doing it during the day. There weren't too many people who were willing to give us a ride. We got a few short hops and finally ended up trying to hitch a ride around Midland. We had just about given up when a speeding car screeched to a halt and we happily hopped aboard.

We were both in the back seat. There was a girl in the back already and she immediately plopped in Maurice's lap. In about 30 seconds we saw that the occupants of the car were extremely drunk. The driver was a young man and his girlfriend was in the front with him. All three people had been drinking for a long time before they picked us up. The driver was trying to knock down any country mailboxes he could find with his car. I didn't try to argue about what the impacts with the mailboxes were doing to the car but tried to get Maurice's attention in order to see just what we could do to get out of this pretty obvious death trap. Maurice was pretty busy trying to breathe with the girl's tongue stuck down his throat and it was hard to get his attention.

We hadn't been in the car for any longer than just a few minutes when the driver tried to take a very sharp corner at a very high rate of speed. The corner was actually an acute angle and the driver was trying to turn on the outside of the acute angle. One of the tires blew out with a loud bang and the car began to tumble.

I can remember being very disoriented and hearing a number of very loud bangs as the car tumbled. It didn't roll as much as it tumbled. I can remember gritting my teeth as hard as I could, tasting dirt in my mouth and wishing the whole thing would please stop. I can remember pain. I guess that I'm a compulsive "counter" as I can remember at least five big bangs before I passed into oblivion.

Some time later I remember waking up and feeling a lot of both pain and pressure. I couldn't move. I couldn't open my eyes, as they felt full of dirt. I couldn't free my arms as they were stuck underneath something so I couldn't rub my eyes. My neck and back hurt a lot. I could feel something underneath me that was moving a little bit and I could smell gasoline. A lot of gasoline. The thought of fire entered my mind, doing nothing to calm me. Oh, God, don't let me burn!

Apparently I was in and out of consciousness a lot because Maurice said that we weren't discovered for quite some time. Maurice had been thrown clear of the wreckage, which ended up in a culvert or ditch by the side of the road. Maurice had climbed out to the road and tried to flag down a passing motorist. Finally he was successful and people started to congregate.

I became aware of a flashlight shining on my closed eyes. Apparently I didn't look too good as I heard someone yell, "We can't do anything for this poor bastard". I immediately yelled back, "You can get me out of here." The next yell was for help in removing the body of the car from my body.

Several people rocked the car off of me enough so that someone could pull me from under the wreck. With each rock and roll of the car the pain increased. As they moved the car they discovered the girl who had been in the back seat. She was pinned underneath me. That was what I had felt moving. Both of us were finally extricated.

For some reason the people who pulled me from the wreck insisted that I stand up. I was very weak from blood loss and couldn't stand on my own. Two people got on either side of me and supported me as I slumped. Apparently they had never attended any first aid courses. I was blood soaked from severe lacerations on my neck and back. When an ambulance and the immediate responders arrived they thought that my neck had been broken. If that had been true the helpful Samaritans could have sentenced me to a life as a paraplegic.

All of the occupants of the car were transported to a local hospital. I passed out several times. I had lost a lot of blood. When I got to the emergency room they cut off most of my bloody clothing. It was pretty well useless anyway. I begged them to try and save my new buckskin fringed shirt. I had saved for weeks to come up with the money for the shirt, which was made from deerskin. The effort was wasted. The shirt was ruined.

The hospital notified my parents. As you can imagine, they were overjoyed to be called up at three in the morning and told that their son was critical in a hospital in Midland, Michigan. They got to the hospital as soon as possible. Later on Dad told me that he was happy that they had seen me before they had seen the wrecked car. It was a total loss and had been broken into three pieces.

I was in the hospital for three days and then released. Every cell in my body ached but I had been extremely lucky. No bones had been broken but I had a lot of "internal injuries", mainly bruising.

Maurice had a lot of bruising but that was the extent of his injuries. The other three occupants had been severely cut. The driver barely survived. No one died. God had been looking out for us all, the good, the bad and the extremely dumb.

That fall I attended college again. Initially I had decided that I would become a Chemical Engineer. Accordingly I was on an Engineering curriculum and was taking a lot of Chemistry. It was a heavy load. I was like many other college kids with a lot of ambition and no money. After a year of school I decided to get a job with one of the many automotive assembly shops that abounded in the Flint, Michigan area. I figured that I could work at night and attend school by day. It was a good plan and only had one flaw. It did not allow for any sleep time. I stuck to the plan for two semesters and my one goal during that whole time seemed to be looking for a place to sleep.

I had found a job at the Albert-Champion Spark Plug Factory, AKA A.C. Spark Plug. My job was challenging from the viewpoint of a garden snail. It entailed working with injection machines that made items for spark plugs and miscellaneous small flashings for the G. M. cars. It was boring in the extreme. To my delight I found that a classmate of mine from college, a beautiful lady in my speech and debate class, was doing the same thing I was. She was working at night in order to make some extra money. She didn't really need the money as her family was relatively well off but she was there, nonetheless. I could have easily fallen in love with her and may well have done so if the age difference between us had not intruded. OK, I'll admit it. I did fall in love with her and have fond memories of her to this day. We shared goals and attitudes. She was wonderful. She made the dull time spent in the automotive shop a lot more interesting. Soon we were sharing rides and eating our lunch together. She had a boy friend, of course. He was a student at the General Motors Technical Institute in Flint that groomed people for jobs at any of the several G.M. plants that abounded in and around Flint. He was going to become a general manager for one of the automotive shops. Mardi was going to marry him and raise several young workers for General Motors. It sounded very insular to me but then what did I know? I was just a kid. In spite of Mr. Wonderful, Mardi and I spent many wonderful times necking before we repaired to our separate homes. Apparently I had gotten over my inferiority complex and had no problems necking with that wonderful lady. I guess I'll always have a soft spot for Mardi and I sincerely hope that her fondest dreams have come true.

One day a foreman told me that I had a new job. I was supposed to check out in the metal injection part of the plant. G.M. needed someone to run one of the big overhead metal pots that were used to fill the metal injection machines with molten metal in the foundry portion of the plant. I had no reservations about the job as I had long ago figured that I could do just about anything that was required of me. The shop foreman ran me through the requirements of the job and then checked me out on the job itself. The plant had a large number of injection mold machines that made castings for things like front and rear grills, headlight housings and all kinds of small castings for interior and exterior accessory metal housings for cars. The metal was made of an aluminum/zinc alloy and was initially liquid. It was tapped by the alloy boy (me) in large half-ton ladles and conducted via an overhead rail system to each injection machine where it was poured into the reservoir of that machine.

My job was to get the liquid metal into the ladle and conduct it to the machines. The job entailed trying to set up a siphon in a curved pipe so as to allow the molten metal to flow into the big ladle. It normally took several tries. Once the ladle was full I had to run it overhead via a remote module to each injection machine. Then I had to tip the ladle so as to fill up the machine's reservoir. It was hard work and made for stomach-gripping times. I was burned every day. I had a suit of heavy cloth and a facemask but still I got burned on my ears and the top of my head. The whole place looked like a Dante's Inferno with fires cropping out every so often in various places and smoke hanging around as if a volcano had just erupted. One day a black girl who was supposed to be on the assembly line got lost in the plant and wandered into the foundry. I saw her looking wide-eyed at a few fires that had just erupted on the floor along with the chug-chug of the injection molding machines and heard her say, "Mothafuck, what am I doing in this place?" I sort of felt the same way.

The pay was good or seemed so, so I kept on with the job. It was onerous but nice if you figured that you could get out of work at 7:00 in the morning, have a banana split and go to bed to awake around 3 o'clock. Of course my sleeping time was constantly interrupted by having to attend classes. It was nice if the ambient noise around the neighborhood would allow you to sleep.

I had met an old time buddy from junior high school named Ron Gallock. He had a job on one of the injection mold machines. I used to kid and joke with him during the evening shift and we would eat lunch together. Ron wasn't interested in college at all and felt that the injection mold machine was an end job for him.

One night as I was filling the machine reservoirs I heard a different noise on the floor. Normally the injection machines would make a noise like "chug-chug". This time the "chug-chug" didn't stop. It kept up continually. I was startled and glanced around rapidly. Finally I saw what the problem was. One of the machines had malfunctioned and had allowed the injection of the molten metal into the die without the die being closed. The result was that the molten metal was pouring into the die under pressure just like a volcano. Molten metal was spraying around the place like a fountain. Inside the fountain was my buddy, Ron, who was now covered with metal and was jumping up and down, screaming. I was horrified. I screamed, "Ron, run this way, run this way, NOW!" He heard me and

ran to me. He was whimpering and his hair was on fire. I beat the
fire out. His face was a mask. Metal covered every inch of his face
and neck. I didn't know how to help him. Another worker beat me
aside as I tried to peel the metal off of his face and yelled, "Leave
him the fuck alone! If you peel the metal you'll scar him for life".
I dropped back and looked on with horror. Soon the emergency
people came on line and Ron was whisked off to an emergency ward
at a local hospital.

The incident had scared me and I didn't want to work in the
foundry zone any longer. I told the supervisor that I was going to
quit and he asked me to reserve my judgment for later.

When I could do so I visited Ron in the hospital. He was a mess.
The staff had removed every mirror from his room. His face was
like a mask with every inch covered with a bright red scab. His eyes
looked out from the mask like holes in a real mask. He was on drugs
to keep him stable. The pain must have been awesome. His hair had
been burned back so that he looked like a middle-aged man. He
could talk but had to stay in his bed. He told me that his eyes had
been saved by the safety glasses that he wore. The wearing of safety
glasses was mandatory in the whole plant. The glasses were fused
with the molten metal and looked more like a die for glasses than
glasses themselves. The A.C. Sparkplug Division of General Motors
kept them and displayed them in their safety presentations until the
plant was finally closed down. He had been fortunate to be wearing
those glasses. Quite a few employees wouldn't wear the glasses if
they could get by with doing so. I had been one of those. No longer!

While I was visiting him a lady passed by looking for a relative
who was in the same hospital. She mistakenly entered Ron's room
and as soon as she saw him she made a horrible face as he startled
her with the way he looked. She only uttered one word and that
sounded like, "Ugh" before she ran out of his room. I felt badly as a
result of the episode and I'm sure that Ron felt the same. He said, "I
guess that I look pretty bad, huh?" I said a few things that obviously
didn't put him at rest but I really couldn't think of anything to say
other than that. He did look like a mess.

Pretty soon the lady came back into the room. She obviously had taken time to think about what she had done and had composed herself. She told Ron that she was sorry for the outburst and that he didn't look "all that bad", etc. It was a good try but it didn't work. Ron pretty well knew how bad he looked by now.

I never went back to the injection mold job. I had been burned enough by the splashing of the molten metal and wanted nothing more to do with the foundry. General Motors offered to allow me to come back to work in any area of work. I declined to do so. They offered to work with me with psychologists. I declined. I was through with G.M. I wanted nothing more to do with them. Finally G.M. offered me a job in an assembly line area. I accepted. The job was too easy. All you had to do was to push several buttons in order to accomplish the job. An idiot could do it. I excelled.

The United Auto Worker's Union came around and told me that I could only fulfill a certain amount of "pieces" of work per night. The edict seemed right. It didn't task us too much and we didn't have to work too hard. That was important. I soon learned that if I worked hard early on I could slough off later on. I could work hard for around seven hours and then relax for one. That was OK according to the Union. It wouldn't do to work harder than the slowest person on the line. I was reminded of the kid who wanted me to work slower when I was employed at the grocery store.

The way I relaxed after I had fulfilled my "quota" according to the Union was to climb to a higher area of the plant and sleep in a "nest" that had been made by a prior worker in the girders that held up the roof of the plant. It was sort of like sleeping with lower order humanoids, like the great apes. Sleeping in that place satisfied some sort of primitive brain stem need. The nest was made by papering an area with cotton shop towels. It was a nice place to sleep and I enjoyed it a lot. I thought that the Union edict was not right but when you are in a situation where you are either right or in extremis you do what you have to do at that time according to the gorilla that is running the show. To do otherwise is to adopt an attitude of "what the hell" and allow the situation to take over, which is to allow the gorilla to do whatever he wishes to do. Bad deal! That was not my finest hour and I was never proud of buckling under the union's edicts.

So the job was nice but not what I wanted for the rest of my life. I talked with my buddy, Mardi, and she confirmed what I thought, that the job was a dead end thing and didn't pay anything anyway. Mardi was neat. She seemed to have a handle on things I hadn't thought about. I listened to her. I kept on trucking at the Junior College in Flint.

One day I simply had it with both the job and the college. I had been going to school in the day and working at A.C. Sparkplug at night. That left little time for sleep and I can remember only looking for a place to crash and sleep during that time period. Finally I had enough and quit both the job and the college course leading to a degree in chemical engineering.

I think that I spent the next month sleeping. I had a large sleep deficit to make up. Finally I came to the realization that I had to do something, anything, to keep body and soul together so I determined to find a job that I could stomach for the rest of my life. I landed a job with Coert's Glass and Paint Company. They needed painters to paint a large security fence around the Buick Motor Division. The fence was miles long and it took a squad of painters all summer to get the job finished. The method of applying the paint (rust oleum) was by a roller that spattered the paint all over the place including the person applying it. I was covered with paint all summer. In addition and in my ignorance I worked without any shirt and, as a result, became as brown as a nut. I was proud of my color but later on in life I had to put up with a bevy of "freckles" all over my back as a result of the skin damage I sustained.

The crew members I worked with were basic people. I learned about their forays with whores and their conquests with regular women. The topics of conversation were either about females, scatology, male genitals, or the "boss", who was greatly feared. It was a lesson in applied living from a different perspective.

One of my favorite co-workers was a man from Holland who had come to the United States in an effort to find a job that would support his family that he had left back in that country. It was always interesting to hear him talk about his country and how it differed from my own.

Another of the work crew was from Iceland. Everyone called him "Icey". He could speak only rudimentary English and his favorite phrase sounded something like "Fockin' Helevita". I could never decipher exactly what that meant.

Another poor soul had an ailment that necessitated that he cough every thirty seconds or so. It was irritating to some of the other crew members but wasn't exactly anything that would really bother anyone. It became an item of humor for the rest of the crew. They christened him "the dog" since his coughs sounded a little like a bark. I can remember Vim, the Dutchman, asking, "Yeisus Christus, ver iss de dok".

It made for an interesting summer and broadened my practical education a lot.

When that summer was over I signed on with a company that said that it would put employers and prospective job seekers together. They steered me toward a printing plant in Flint named Perry Printing Company. Perry was looking for a bindery foreman replacement. The job description was for an apprenticeship that would last for four years prior to becoming a certified foreman. It seemed like an interesting job so I signed on.

The job entailed setting up jobs relating to the printing industry for approximately thirty or forty women and overseeing the accomplishment of those jobs. The jobs were all about everything that had to be accomplished after things had been printed on paper, that is, collating, cutting, drilling for holes, gluing for books, folding, stacking and binding for shipping, etc. The bindery did everything needed for printed material other than the actual printing. The job was exasperating. All of the women who worked in the bindery were older than I was and they resented my presence. They also knew that I was a "newbie" and generally wouldn't acknowledge that I was the representative of the foreman who let me do any of the work I seemed to be able to do. I did this for a few years. Meanwhile I attended the Naval Reserve Surface Division faithfully each month. The Navy seemed to give me an anchor into whatever was meaningful at the time. I loved it.

Finally the owner of Perry Printing called me to his office and offered me a job as a printing salesman. The job also included an offer to pay for college in that I could be a college attendee for half the day and work for the company for the other half. My pay would be for a full day regardless. It was an extremely good offer and I accepted it immediately. The position of printing salesmen at Perry was a plumb. They had lots of perks and lots of freedom along with very good paychecks. They were part of the elite in the company. At that time in my life I didn't know that I was not constitutionally suited to become a salesman. I paid attention to the college part of the deal but was a little at sea as regards the other part. I had long known that I was not a salesman as such. I had a hard time "smoozing" anyone. The real salesmen at the company were good guys. Everyone loved them. They seemed to have a rapport with everyone. I tended to be withdrawn and introspective. I could be very friendly but couldn't be false in any way. I wasn't a good innate salesman.

I could have foretold the outcome of the deal that had been offered to me. It wasn't hard. Hell, if anyone would have asked me if I thought that I was a good salesman I could have told them that the answer was "no". I've always said that I couldn't sell a gold brick for three dollars. Finally the company decided to rid itself of me based on a "work in progress inventory" that I had to work on. The ostensible reason to "fire" me was that I had not reported the appropriate amounts of work done on some of the work-in-progress items. In actuality I had asked the senior salesmen what would have been charged on those jobs and I reported those amounts rather than the "book" prices.

The owner called me into his office and castigated me at length. I had no retort knowing that the result was to fire me and that everything else was fluff. I stood mute while he ripped me from one side to another in his attempts to make himself feel good about the termination and finally he told me that I wasn't wanted in the company any more. OK, I left after saying goodbye to some of the people that I had made friends with and that was that.

Thinking back I can honestly say that I didn't want to be a salesman for a printing company. There simply had to be something else I could do. I used to think about the guys who hired on to the printing company as salesmen and I felt/feel sorry for them. Becoming a salesman for a printing company in Flint, Michigan is tantamount to what General George Patton talked about when he spoke of "shoveling shit in Louisiana". Who wants to do that?

I had always been affiliated with the Naval Reserve in Flint. The Surface Division 9-95 was interesting and rewarding. When I was in high school a lot of the boys were enlisting in the National Guard. I tried to enlist along with everyone else. Since I was "underage" Dad had to sign for me. He refused saying that I could join the Navy or the Marines but definitely not the Army or the National Guard. Finally I went with a few friends who were going to join the Naval Reserve.

When I was introduced to the Naval Reserve the team responsible for induction asked me why I wished to join. I told them that I really would rather have joined the National Guard and they asked me why. I told them that the National Guard had rifles and guns and I could shoot them. The team asked me if I liked shooting big guns. When I readily said that I did the recruiters led me into a large area where there was a twin 20MM anti-aircraft gun set up. They sat me into one of the seats and allowed me to train and point the twin guns at bogus aircraft. It was heady in the extreme. Was that what I wanted to do as far as big guns were concerned? Absolutely! I signed up for a "minority cruise" that evening. A minority cruise was a stint with the Naval Reserve for minors. The parents of the minor had to OK the enlistment before it was legal.

The Naval Reserve was a heady experience. Initially I was a Seaman Recruit. I had to draw several items of uniform and learn how to take care of them. I had to learn how to tie clothing onto laundry lines with laundry stops. The Navy did not recognize clothespins. We had to use clothes stops. Clothes stops were short pieces of line that were used to tie the clothing to a line so that the wind would not blow the clothing away. I had to learn how to roll clothing into rolls that were placed into sea-bags. I attended Navy boot camp at Camp Porter at the Great Lakes Naval Station. I learned how to fight fires in fire-fighting school where the Chief Petty Officer shoved us into the fire while he shouted, "Fight the fucking fire", as we sprayed the water into the fire in our faces. I learned the meaning of fear as the fire tried to burn me. I can still remember the sound of the fire as it roared and the sound of the Chief as he shouted, "Get in there. Fight the fucking fire. Spray that water. You can't come out until the fire is out." I learned about gas attacks when I had to go into a gas-filled room and take off my mask. After the mask was off I had to stand in the gas-filled room, recite my name and serial number and then, only then, was I allowed to exit the room. I learned that the individual wasn't worth much and that the group was important. I learned a lot of things from that school but the most important thing I learned was that the individual wasn't much. The group was everything. The group or whatever you call that group is the critical ganglion that accomplishes the things that need to be accomplished. Think Marines.

I was singularly impressed with the Chief Petty Officer who ran the sick bay. Initially I had to show up there every day in order to get the series of shots that were mandated for each man. In my ignorance I thought that the Chief was a doctor. I mentioned that I would like to be like the Chief and was accordingly assigned to "strike" or study in order to become a hospital corpsman. It was interesting and challenging and I became a Second Class Petty Officer in relatively short order. Most of my active duty stints were spent at the Naval Hospital at Great Lakes, Illinois where I served in the operating rooms and the various labs and hospital wards giving shots, dressing wounds and caring for patients.

Initially, when I had first joined Surface Division 9-95 I had to report to sick bay each week during the meetings I had to attend. The reason was in order to complete the series of shots I had to have that was supposed to protect me from all of the diseases and illnesses a sailor could expect to be exposed to. The shots were a minor inconvenience and, other than making my upper arms sore for a few days, were a non-event. Not everyone viewed the shots in that way.

A Lieutenant who had to have some booster shots apparently feared shots of any type. He showed up one evening and got in the shot line. He kept relinquishing his position in the line for one near the end as if to stave off the inevitable. I was near the end of the line when he took a position directly behind me. I had just gotten a shot in both arms by the two Corpsmen standing on either side of the line when I heard an odd noise. It sounded like "uhhnnnn". I glanced around to my rear just in time to see the Lieutenant topple toward me. He was as stiff as a board with his hands held stiffly by his sides and was falling towards me much as a tree falls when it is finally cut. I was startled and jumped out of the way to avoid being hit by his body.

The Chief Petty Officer saw what was happening and was rising out of his chair behind a desk shouting, "Catch him! Catch him! Goddamn it, catch him!" No one, of course, did and the Lieutenant continued his majestic fall, hitting his chin on the edge of the desk, doing a half-roll onto his back and finally hitting the back of his head on the cement deck with a noise like that of a dropped watermelon. His chin had split open and blood was covering his uniform.

I felt guilty at having not caught the Lieutenant and immediately squatted near him, picking his head off the deck as I did. The Chief Petty Officer screamed, "Leave him the fuck alone!" Startled again, I released the Lieutenant's head which immediately plopped back onto the cement deck with the same watermelon noise once more. This prompted a round of curses from the Chief which took in all of the enlisted men in the sick bay, their immediate families, officers in general, Lieutenants in particular and several deities that I had never heard of.

Later on, when I had occasion to strike for a rating I chose that of Hospital Corpsman. I was relieved to find that the Chief did not remember me or my sterling performance on that memorable evening.

One day I had to go to the Naval Reserve Air Station in Grosse Ile, Michigan in order to get some items of my uniform that were not available at the Surface Division where I was attached. Grosse Ile is on an island just south of Detroit. The name is French. It means "large island". It was an easy hours drive from Flint. I parked my car and was walking toward the "small stores" where uniform items were sold when I saw a lanky looking officer walking along holding a golden flight helmet at his side. He was headed toward what appeared to be a giant airplane parked on what I later learned was the area where planes were parked near the tower and operations center. The plane looked lethal. It had things hung under the wings that looked like bombs. I stopped another enlisted man and asked him what the plane was and who the guy was who was walking toward the plane. I was told that the man was the pilot and that the plane was a P2V. The man who offered the information was a crewmember and told me that the "things" under the wings were jet engines and not "bombs". He said that bombs and other things were held in a bomb bay. I was hooked.

When I got back to the Reserve Center I babbled about the plane to the resident station keeper who told me that the Navy had a program that would allow me to become a pilot if I wanted to become one. I was enthralled. Of course I wanted to become one. Who wouldn't? He told me that it was really tough and that few made it that tried. I didn't care. I wanted this more than I had ever wanted anything.

I took a series of tests and soon I was talking to an officer who asked me a lot of questions about why I wanted to become a Navy officer and pilot. Quickly I was notified that I had been accepted for the Naval School, Preflight. My Division Officer, a SRO (Surface Warfare Officer) had to OK my transfer. He was an obese Lieutenant who looked like he might split out his uniform trousers. His fingernails were dirty and broken. He signed my transfer papers with the statement, "You ain't gonna make it, kid, but I'll sign this thing anyhow." So much for a rousing cheer for success.

I was assigned an officer who was supposed to monitor my progress. He told me that I needed a full two years of college before I could qualify for the Preflight School. I needed a couple of classes. I buckled down and soon had the classes under my belt and was ready to attend the Navy's school leading toward becoming a pilot. During that time I married my high school sweetheart, Joan Lane. Why not? I was ready to become a Navy pilot and could look toward a nice paycheck every two weeks.

When I had finished the two college courses I reapplied to the Officer I had been assigned to. He asked me to update my vital records and looked over my shoulder as I did so. When I wrote down that I was married he said, "Hold on. I didn't know that you were married." I responded, "I wasn't the last time I spoke to you. I just got married." He looked strangely at me and said, "Well, congratulations, I guess. The situation has changed a bit though. The program you applied for, as a Naval Aviation Cadet is only open for unmarried people. If you're married then you have to have four years of college and that program is called the Aviation Officer Candidate program. When you get two more years of college come back and see us." And that was that. I was stunned. Why didn't I do my homework? I had just learned about the law of unintended consequences. There was no sense crying about it. I had to get more college under my belt. I resolved to do so. By now I really wanted to be a Naval Aviator.

The next two years were ones of lean times, lots of study time and humble living. My new wife had a job in a bank and that kept us from starvation. I did what I could, delivering messages from doctors and scut work like that. It was a low spot in my life. I had no pride. I felt like the most scurrilous of peons or serfs. We lived in a house trailer in a small trailer park in Flint. It was a nice park but still had the usual social stigmas attached to parks like that. My nearest neighbor was an obese, unusually ugly man called Leroy. He had a large growth over one eye and was friendly but (did I mention it) was extremely ugly. Leroy lived with his obese mother who had advanced diabetes and who could hardly walk. They had an old sofa that they had installed in front of their trailer where they could sit and wave to passers by. I always called the couch a "howdy neighbor" couch as that was what the usual greeting was from either Leroy or his Mom. I tried, usually unsuccessfully, to avoid the pair. They were pleasant but repulsive. I've always felt badly that I didn't interact more with them. I also felt like a "kept man" and that didn't do anything for my self-esteem. I desperately needed a job that brought in money.

I kept my nose to the grindstone as regards my studies. I determined that the quickest way toward a degree was to major in Business Administration. The Bus Ad major seemed too easy to me and so, to salvage my self-esteem, I opted for a double major of Business Administration/Economics with a minor in Psychology. The Psychology was interesting but the Economics studies were terrible in the extreme. The Professor of Economics was an old maid who thought that John Maynard Keynes was some sort of God. I studied Keynesian economics until I thought that I would vomit. The Economics discipline was so taxing that most of the time there were only two people in the whole class. The Professor insisted on teaching in the Socratic method of asking questions of her class. It got so bad that if either of us wished to cut the class we had to ask the permission of the other classmate since, if only one person showed up, he was the total recipient of all of the questions fielded that day.

Much later in life I realized that I had completely wasted my studies of Keynes as he was not only a homosexual but was a Socialist to boot. And he definitely did not have the right answers to economics in general. We are still paying the price for his erroneous economic theories. So much for college. Still, it was a key to my original goal of flying Navy airplanes. I pushed on in order to persevere.

I still had the original scholarship I had been awarded and I used it to the maximum. I carried as many credits as possible and still maintained an A-B average. My goal was, as always, to graduate in order to fly Navy airplanes. In the final year of my collegiate studies I found that I could graduate six months early if I could only carry an extra three credit hours over the maximum. I applied to the college for this waiver and one day I was called to the Dean's office to be read a letter from the board that had considered my request. The letter said, "While we feel that Mr. Landers is fully capable of taking the extra three credit hours and maintaining his A-B average we feel that his outlook is too mercenary. We further feel that he could better profit from staying the full six months in college, taking some extra humanities and thinking about the plight of his fellow man."

When the letter had been read to me I exploded. "Think about the plight of my fellow man"? I yelled, "I only want to fly Navy planes and bomb and strafe my fellow man". The Dean frostily terminated the conversation and I had the extra six months to do. I stubbornly took exactly three credit hours and turned my back on the "humanities". To this day I maintain that the University of Michigan had handed down that decision on the basis of gaining as much money as possible due to the additional credit hours chalked up. It was the old song; talk about lofty things while paying attention to the mundane, i.e., the "bottom line" or money. Since that time I have had no use for academia in general and snooty academic administrators in particular. That is not to say that I disdain learning. I love learning just about anything. I simply have no use for the so-called intelligentsia who administer it.

A few weeks prior to my graduation I notified the Navy about my status, updated my vital statistics and shortly after graduating I was on a Navy SNB, a small twin-engine plane, on my way to the Naval School, Preflight. My wife was left behind in a nice rental apartment. I had left one life and was well on my way to another. I felt fortunate in that I did not have to undergo any tests leading to a life of sitting at some desk in some musty office or, worse, ensconced in some small cubicle embedded in a matrix of other cubicles adding small columns of numbers incessantly and fruitlessly.

A new life awaited me. One of freedom. One that was full of excitement, challenge and hardship but one that promised to be infinitely rewarding. Flying seemed to me to be the culmination of everything I had tried and had successfully accomplished in my life so far. It was somewhat dangerous and that added to the spice of the goal. Someone, somewhere said that the most alive you will ever be is when you are living on the edge of life, where you can never be sure that you will be allowed to live from one minute to another, where nothing is assured and all things are fluid, where chance is king and where your expertise may well be the only thing that keeps you alive. What other challenge can meet this one? There are those who are very satisfied living a humdrum life, playing golf, fishing, mowing the lawn, playing with their children. That is an admirable life and one that is satisfying and rewarding to those who aspire to peace and contentment. Then there are those who aspire to the life of a warrior, who love to test the situation, who live to strive against others or other situations, who love to fight or make war, if you will. Society needs these people to intercede for the peace lovers among us. Everyone has a niche. Mine was not that of a bean counter or a stockbroker. I craved excitement and challenge. I needed the rush of speed, danger, excitement. What other endeavor could give one all of that rolled up into one job? Naval Aviation seemed to be the one thing that could satisfy all requirements.

I finally satisfied all requirements of any of the facilities that required things of me. I had passed the background tests that were required of anyone who had wished to become a Naval Aviator. All of my friends and acquaintances had been interviewed by the government people who do things like this. I was on my way. To celebrate my success I bought a new 1960 Chevrolet convertible in sky blue, a color I thought appropriate. Of course I couldn't take it to Pensacola with me so my wife, Joan, would use it until she could join me in Florida. That was going to take some time. I had no illusions concerning how long my training was going to take or how hard it would be. Joan would stay in a rental apartment in Flint, Michigan until I was quite sure that I would be successful as a Navy pilot. After all, the dropout (read failure) rate for Naval Aviators was somewhere in the 60 or 70 percent rate. I had resolved that I was not going to be counted in the dropout statistics.

The pilots of the SNB, a small twin-engine aircraft, who were taking me to the Naval Air Station, Pensacola, Florida questioned me unceasingly. They reminisced at length about how they had entered the Naval Aviation program. One of the pilots said that he would reenter the program at any time as he loved what had happened to him. The other pilot said that he thought that the first pilot was crazy and that he, personally, would never reenter the program. It was interesting to say the least.

On the way to Pensacola our Navy plane encountered another one. The other Navy plane was crossing our path at right angles, passing from right to left. The other plane was obviously a fighter type. It was much speedier and sleeker than the old SNB. When the other pilot saw us he executed what I later learned was an aileron roll. When the pilot of the SNB saw that he grinned and shook his finger at the other plane. I didn't know, at that time, what the problem was but later on I learned that a plane is not supposed to perform acrobatics on federal airways, even to say "hello" to a kindred spirit.

When the small plane arrived at Pensacola it was an afterthought. The pilots shook our hands and wished us well. I distinctly remember that one of the pilots said, "you poor fucker", before he turned to his plane.

Much later in my military career I had occasion to be present in a survival school for jungle survival wherein not only Navy but also Army people were present. During a roll call most of us answered "Here" or "Yo" when our name was called. One humorous wag called "Present, one each!" It was obvious that he had been in the Supply Corps as the usual way to account for items in the supply system was unique. Groups of items were named after the usual way the items in the group were counted as in "dozen", "gross", "pounds", etc. In each case the items would be designated as "one, dozen" or "five, pounds" or "one, each".

As for me, I was Present, One Each.

Afterward

To the reader:

If you have gotten this far you are to be congratulated. People who read are in short supply today. I've always felt that the ability to read trumps most other abilities and desires in humans. The advent of television has, unfortunately, put reading on the backburner of history. The advent and popularity of the internet has not curtailed the necessity of being able to read but it has depressed the reading of books. An ancillary sorrow to all of this is that any good author has to have been able to read extensively and thus the lack of a desire to read has derogated the publishing of good authors who would have, arguably, produced many hours of enjoyable reading for those who love to experience other things and other lives vicariously.

I do not pretend to list myself in that august group of wonderful writers. I write because it gives me pleasure. If my humble offerings give you any pleasure or recall then I have been immensely successful.

If you liked this book and would like to know just what happened to "Eddie" I can recommend my book Smooth (The Development and Formation of a Naval Aviator). The best and the most economical way to access Smooth is to write to me at:

Edward Landers
1050 North Spring Street
Elgin, Illinois 60120
Or email me at:
ASWEX@comcast.net

Smooth takes the reader through Naval Aviation as it was during 1960 to 1968 from the Naval School, Preflight to three different squadrons, AEWBARRONPAC, VP11 and VP30. $28.95 plus $4.00 shipping.

The author is currently working on another book that takes the reader from the author's separation from active duty to flying in the Naval Reserve and with Northwest Airlines. This book is planned to be published in 2013. If you liked the first two books you will love the third. Contact the author in order to be notified when the book is available.

Thanks for reading my book. I sincerely hope that it gave you many hours of pleasure.

Edward Landers